A PAINTER
OF OUR TIME

*Available from Pantheon
**Available from the Pantheon Modern Writers series

JOHN BERGER

·····················

A PAINTER
OF OUR TIME

WITH A NEW AFTERWORD
BY THE AUTHOR

PANTHEON BOOKS   NEW YORK

Library of Congress Cataloging-in-Publication Data

Berger, John.
A painter of our time / John Berger.
p.   cm.
Reprint. Originally published: London : Writers and Readers Pub.
Cooperative, 1976.
ISBN 0-679-72271-8
I. Title.
[PR6052.E564P3 1989]
823′.914—dc 19   88-25564
CIP

Manufactured in the United States of America

First Pantheon Edition

In no society is any product the exclusive result of one man's effort. Many contribute. I would like to acknowledge in particular the contributions of the following to this book – contributions by way of example, criticism, encouragement and quite straightforward, practical services of help: Victor Anant, the late Frederick Antal, Anya Bostock, John Eskell, Peter de Francia, Renato Guttuso, Peter Peri, Wilson Plant, Friso and Vica Ten Holt, Garith Windsor, and my own parents.

Life will always be bad enough
for the desire for something better
not to be extinguished in men

MAXIM GORKY

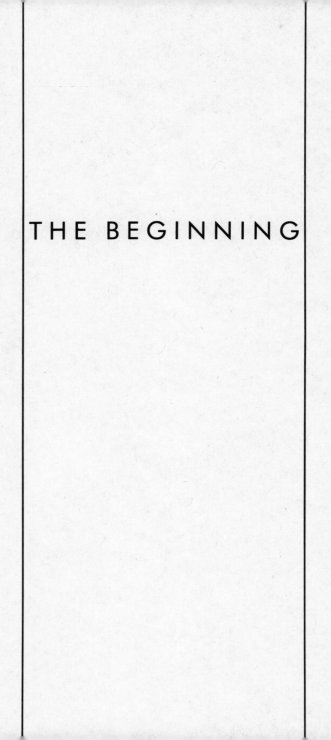

THE BEGINNING

On the door was a strip of metal foil with 'Janos Lavin' printed on it. It had come from one of those machines on railway-stations into which you put a penny – or is it now sixpence? – to print so many letters. Bureaucrats should always use them when writing their speeches. I had the key, and so I let myself in.

The place – it was a large studio – felt uninhabited. Everything was there in its usual position, but one could tell that nothing had been moved or used for at least a week.

I had come with no very definite purpose in mind. I told myself that I would just check up, see that the skylight wasn't leaking on to anything, and maybe look at some of the paintings again. I was too mystified and shocked to start making plans.

Having let myself in, I did not know what to do. All the old life had gone. I strode up and down, looking at everything as though I were some kind of inspector. That was useless. I must take it easier. I would make myself a cup of coffee. The grinder was fixed to the wall at the kitchen end of the studio. The coffee-tin was in the kitchen. The water had not been cut off – or perhaps one couldn't cut the water off without cutting it off from the other studios as well. On the draining-board there was a tea-pot with tea leaves in it and an unwashed cup: a sign of shock and hurried departure. There was also on the window-sill a jam-jar of water with half a dozen brushes soaking in it: a sign, to any painter who values his brushes – and anyway they are expensive enough – of neglect.

The whole place was very quiet, as if I were hearing an accumulated absence of sound. While the kettle was boiling, I went and sat in one of the wicker chairs in the studio. It went on creaking after I had settled in it and was sitting quite still. Skin had formed over all the mounds of paint on the painting table. There was no smell of either oil or turps. I tried to imagine

Janos suddenly appearing. I could not. One of his berets was hanging on the back of the door. The wheel of the etching press over in the alcove looked as permanently stationary as a mill-wheel whose stream has long dried up.

Everything was the same, yet to my eyes everything looked different; everything except what the studio was full of – the painted canvases. Such of these as faced outwards appeared exactly as they had done before. It was a typical London autumn afternoon, but even in that muted light their colours remained strong and resonant. The huge figures in *The Games* canvas, that leant along the whole length of one wall, looked certain and unalterable. Never before had I realized so vividly and personally what all our talk about unity of 'form' and 'style' meant. By virtue of these qualities, this canvas now had an independent life. Around it were the personal effects the meaning of which had been transformed by recent events. Not so the painting. It was already beginning to outlast the circumstances that had given rise to its being painted. On to everything else in the studio except the paintings I was able to project my own feeling of confusion and loss. In their own way the paintings were as independent as the sky on a day of national tragedy.

The kettle whistled. Against the frosted window, over the sink in the kitchen, was a piece of mirror. Waiting for the coffee to filter through, I gazed idly into it. Here Janos shaved, and Diana, if she was in too much of a hurry to go up to the bedroom, did her hair and touched up her lips. I thought of their faces. His, for all its sensitivity, rather like a potato that has just been dug out of the earth, brown and dirty looking in a wholesome way; hers, like a fine china cup – with a cherry pattern on it to represent her lips. Beside the mirror was a razor. If he was alive, did he now have a beard? He hated Bohemianism. But he was nearly sixty, and a beard would have become his years and his appearance of always having something on his mind. He never looked passive. Even if he was sitting back in one of the wicker chairs smoking a cigarette, he always gave the impression he was working something out – probably he wasn't, but he looked like it. When did he work out what he had now done?

I took my cup of coffee back into the studio, and sat in the corner behind the painting table. From here he usually worked, with the easel at an angle placed towards the centre of the room. On a shelf was another piece of mirror which probably originally belonged to the same one as the shaving piece. This one was for squinting at the canvas in. Except for the actual painting implements – the palette knives, the easel and the bundles of brushes – every other object in this corner was an improvised scrap. The painting table was an old desk with the drawers missing. There were a dozen cups without handles – for oil or turps or size or varnish. There were broken plates used as temporary, small palettes. Beneath the brown paper bags of colours, all stained with their own bright dusts, was a cornerless marble slab from an old washstand on which the dusts were worked into paint. There were old shirts and sheets stuffed under the table, yellowed newspapers stacked on the floor. There was a broken bucket half filled with matches and cigarette stubs.

Such is the working 'furniture' of nine studios out of ten. What distinguishes one from another are the objects, the photographs, the personal tokens with which the particular painter chooses to surround himself. These are talismans for good painting. Bits of tree trunk, fragments of coloured glass, an old poster, a few of his own drawings, a photograph of Miss Universe next to a Leonardo drawing of a plant, a seashell – the variety and combinations are endless. I have seldom seen a studio which has not had its collection.

I looked at the wall beside my chair. It now seemed rather like going through a man's wallet in order to identify him. Not that there was anything there which I hadn't seen dozens of times before. I was almost as familiar with this studio as with my own living-room. I had imagined that I knew Janos well – far better than any of his few other English friends. We were intimates. But now the unexpected had forced me to realize how little I had known of him, and I looked at the scraps of paper pinned to the edges of the shelves and to the wall, in the vague hope that they would give me a clue to what I had not known, to what I had missed.

There were several photographs of athletes in action – hurdlers, skiers, divers. There was a picture postcard of the Eiffel Tower. There was a photograph of himself with some other students at Budapest University in 1918. He had originally intended to be a lawyer. He did not seriously begin painting until his early twenties, when he was in Prague – having been forced to leave Hungary after the overthrow of the Soviet revolutionary government of 1919. There was another photograph of about a dozen people at a studio party in his own Berlin studio in the late twenties. In the background one could see some of his own paintings, which were then abstract. There was a torn piece of paper with MAY I OFFER YOU MY HEARTFELT CONGRATULATIONS written in block capitals upon it. He had pinned this up about a year ago, and I had never asked him to explain it. He was a forbidding man to question about himself, and he seldom referred to what is called 'his emotional life'. One had the impression that he considered that in this respect too many people wasted too much time over details. Probably this was a wrong impression.

There was a reproduction of Poussin's *The Court of Flora*, another of Léger's *Les Constructeurs* and another of Van Gogh's *Potato-Eaters*. He quite often changed these, pinning up something new when he came across it. There was always, however, a Poussin. High up on the wall there was one of his own drawings – a portrait head of Diana, which he must have done soon after they were married, for in it she looks like a young ballet dancer. Under the drawing was written *Rosie*, which was Janos's pet-name for her. Hers for him was *Jimmy*. Thus they hid some of their differences.

Written on the wall with a paint brush was a quotation from Éluard – '*Je ne regrette rien, j'avance.*' Beneath was a telephone number, which I recognized as Susan's.

There were also several newspaper photographs – but nothing in this opened-out wallet was yielding any new information. I was only being reminded of what I already knew.

When the telephone rang, I jumped so much that I spilt some of my coffee. I went down to the other end of the studio under the balcony to answer it. It was the Malvern Gallery wanting to speak to Janos about the price of one of his paintings. Obviously no one had told them, and so I stalled and said Janos was away for a few days. It probably meant they were selling another painting. That made a total of ten in a fortnight, and all of them large and expensive. I looked round at the hundreds of canvases stacked along the walls, even taking up space in this, the domestic end of the 50-foot studio, and the irony of it made me furious. Not the grand life and death irony of it, but the irony of it measured out in thousands of daily irritations no grander than chilblains, and no less painful.

I clambered up the stairs to the balcony in order to look into the two bedrooms leading off it. This was Diana's part of their living space – it is impossible to call one of these studios a home: those who live in them have rejected the concept. Although here nothing was pinned to the walls, the furniture and furnishings were themselves autobiographical: the eighteenth-century dressing-table in the bedroom, the silver-framed photographs, the bow chest-of-drawers, the decanter on the balcony table, and a dozen other objects, had all clearly come from a house in the country where they had been polished by a succession of house-maids for several generations. They had reflected – literally – a way of life. Here in this cramped space they looked like a few possessions that had hastily been packed into a wagon by their owner fleeing from her home. On the floor in the spare bedroom was a dark, mouldy-looking dispatch-case. Once this had been Diana's token of emancipation in the new life she had chosen. Everything was in order. And I clambered back down the ladderlike stairs.

It was cold without the stove burning, and even if it hadn't been, there was no point in staying. I decided to go. I washed up, and then, passing the bookshelf, I remembered that Janos had had my copy of Diderot translations, which I should need. I looked along the shelf for it. Underneath the shelf on the floor were wedged dozens of red-covered sketch-books. On an impulse I took out the only one which was not jammed in. Janos was always rather cagey about his working drawings. I flicked the pages. To my surprise there was no drawing in it; it was full of writing. I looked more closely. A few sentences were in English and French, but most were in another language – presumably Hungarian. I then noticed that many of the para-graphs were dated. Three years ago. Last year. I rushed to the last page of writing. It had been written twelve days before. Janos had kept a journal.

I sat on the floor and started searching for an entry which I could read in order to get some idea of how it was written. I could not find one. I could only recognize names here and there.

I was both excited and appalled. Excited because I had come to the studio in the vague, half-conscious hope of being able to understand more, to discover something, and this was a more positive discovery than I would have thought possible. Appalled because a mystery was ending.

I would now learn exactly how this man whom I had loved as a friend had eluded me, and therefore how I had failed him.

I forgot about my Diderot. I wanted to go straightaway. I gave a last look round the studio. The paintings did look different now, but only because it was getting dark. Given this light, they would always look like this. The athletes in *The Games* would always be heroes. Tucking the book under my arm, I hurried out. I wanted to be amongst people again, but, as so often in London, all but the main streets were deserted.

Looking back on it today, it surprises me a little that I didn't hesitate then, that I didn't wonder whether I was justified in taking the book away with me. But I didn't.

What I did hesitate about for a whole year was whether or not to publish Janos's journal. A Hungarian friend first read the book out loud to me. It was a humiliating experience. But as I recovered from my own personal shocks, I began to realize what a remarkable document I had in my hands. My friend, who prefers to remain anonymous, made a written translation into rough English. When I read this, I saw even more clearly how much the book revealed; it amounted to a *Portrait of the Artist as an Emigré*, and today in one sense or another most artists are *émigrés*.

I will not bother the reader with all the arguments I had with myself about the rights and wrongs of making what follows public. Finally, I decided it was right to do so, but that, in order to complete the picture of these four years of a painter's life, it was necessary to have also a commentary of background facts. This I have tried to write. I have also, with the help of my friend, tried to polish the translation. Naturally, I have changed most of the names.

THE BOOK

1952

In this sketch-book I shall make no drawings. It is a long time since I have reserved a book for comments. In Berlin I used to note down remarks and quotations for later use in lectures, polemics, arguments. But in this one I shall stick to myself. I have now become political history: I need not record it as an exterior phenomenon. Though that is not the reason for my reserving this book for these notes. I need to see myself again. In the past I recognized myself in the critical events in which I took part. But now for ten years in this secluded and fortunate country my life has been eventless. I have worked. But it is not the creation of a painting which constitutes an event: the event is the way it is welcomed by others. I do not regret that my life has been eventless. In a certain sense, I am grateful. I have experienced my share. And now I require all my energy for my work. Such a state of affairs, however, leads to a loss of a proper sense of time. We measure time by events. And without them, you can become careless with time. Writing these occasional notes, and perhaps even re-reading them, will make me guard time more jealously. Consequently, I shall work harder. As one grows older, every moment passes to one between the twin sentinels of gratitude and fear. Strictly speaking, the fear that it may not arrive precedes the gratitude that it has. But the process is so fast that they seem simultaneous, whilst the moments follow one another so quickly that normally we acknowledge neither the gratitude nor the fear. Only sometimes we can slow them down, and so notice the precariousness of our position. On these pages I will slow them down.

Janos was not given to talking about abstract themes — or, anyway, not to me. Naturally he had his abstract words and, like all of

us, *he gave them his own intonation. For example, he had a particu-*
lar way of saying the word justice. He spoke of justice as if it were a
presence – as you might speak of a girl who had just left the room or
the town. But I remember that on one occasion he did speak about
the problem of Time in a rather different way from the above entry.
'There is something even more fundamental than sex or work,' he
said. 'The great universal, human need to look forward. Take the
future away from a man, and you have done something worse than
killing him.'

JANUARY 12

In front of me is a rose in a tumbler. Susan brought it. As it
unfolds, it turns like the hub of an air-screw; each petal as it
falls back appears to propel it a few degrees farther round – the
petals as blades.

I cannot paint flower-pieces, any more than I can paint
dancers dancing or actors acting. The subject is too obviously
there.

Susan was one of Janos's ex-students from the art school at
which he taught two days a week. She admired his work and
occasionally posed for him. She was not his mistress.

JANUARY 14

A student asked me what century I would choose to live in – as a
painter. I replied today. It is the only answer possible. You soon
give up wishing you had a different kind of mother when you
have to keep her.

I first met Janos about two years before he began this journal, at
the National Gallery. (It is remarkable how, for those who suffer
a desire for art, so much does begin and end in it.) We were both
standing near the Goya portrait of Doña Isabel when a girl art
student strode up to look at it. She had loose dark hair which she
flicked back from her face by tossing her head, and she wore a tight
black skirt – this was before the fashion for jeans – which looked as
though it were held up like a towel and might at any moment come
apart but without in the least disconcerting her. She stood in front
of the painting, leaning slightly backwards with one hand on her
hip, and so echoing quite unconsciously the pose of Doña Isabel

18

herself. I noticed Janos, a tall man in a huge black overcoat, looking at her and then at the painting with considerable amusement. He glanced at me, still smiling. His eyes in their much-creased sockets were very bright. He looked an energetic sixty. I smiled back. When the girl strode off into the next gallery, we both went up to the Goya. 'The living and the undying,' he said in a deep, noticeably foreign voice. 'What a choice!'

Closer to him now, I could study more carefully the expression of his face. It was an urban face, experienced, strained, travelled: but it could still register surprise. It was the opposite of polished. Given the context, it was obvious that he was a painter, and his hands were stained with printing ink; yet in another context one might have guessed that he was a gardener or park-keeper. He was clearly a solitary and had clearly never in his life had a secretary. He had a large nose with hairs coming out of the nostrils; a thick but drawn mouth; a bald brow and top to his head; and a thrusting crooked chin. He stood very upright.

When I inquired what his name was and he told me, I just recognized it. I dimly remembered having seen a book of anti-Nazi war drawings published seven or eight years before. They had struck me because unlike most such drawings they were not expressionist; if, however, I had thought any more about the artist, I had assumed that he had gone back to the Continent. Later, when I used to mention his name to people in the art world, the majority looked blank. He was known to a few isolated groups: to one or two left-wing intellectuals, to a few Berlin émigrés, to the Hungarian Embassy, to a number of young painters whom he had met personally, and – presumably – to M.I.5.

To those who may think it remarkable that, although in the late twenties Janos had a considerable reputation in Berlin and had had a book published in London at the end of the war, he was in the fifties virtually forgotten, I must emphasize three facts.

The London art world is extremely parochial, and such foreign artists as are admitted into it nearly all have Parisian reputations. To take just one other example: Egon Schiele, a young Viennese artist of the First World War, whose work is certainly as striking as Gaudier Brezka's or Modigliani's, is still absolutely unknown in this country. Second. The art world, not so dissimilar from the film world, moves forward at a great pace, always searching for new *names, and inevitably forgetting those who do not reappear every year. Who now discusses Nevinson? Third. Fashion – for those who haven't already a reputation – is exclusive; those who do not conform to the latest style are considered dated or uninteresting. This even affects the assessment of Old Masters; before the war the Tiepolos were beyond the aesthetic pale, now their works are studied and bought avidly. It is not difficult to imagine how even more completely and arbitrarily this exclusiveness of the latest fashion dominates the evaluation of unknown contemporaries.*

In these respects Janos's position was in no way special. He was typical of dozens, or even hundreds, of other painters and sculptors.

About a year after I met him, he did hold a small exhibition in a basement gallery in Kensington. At the time I advised him against it. The gallery was run by a Viennese woman covered with jade. She gave exhibitions almost entirely to foreigners, in an attempt perhaps to reconstruct for herself the cosmopolitan eventfulness of Vienna. But because she had no discrimination whatsoever and showed the work of anybody who could pay for the gallery or with whom she wanted an affair, no one ever visited her exhibitions. The whole thing was no more than a hobby, a kind of latter-day dowdy salon for her. When I explained this to Janos he smiled in his most stupidly ironic manner and, waving his hand at the studio walls with hundreds of canvases stacked against them, said, 'It will, please notice, give me more space for at least one month.' So he had his exhibition. There were no reviews. And only two water-colours were sold to an American woman friend of the gallery owner. Since Janos had had to frame many of the pictures, transport them to the gallery and pay for the printing of the catalogue as well as the rent, he was about £50 out of pocket.

JANUARY 19

Last night, after the day's teaching, I worked late on the etching of *The Waves and Gulls*. Today I drew from this etching in preparation for the painting. It is to be a large one. The canvas is on the easel now, as large and white as a sheet that has never been slept in. My paintings have become larger and larger as I have grown older. As a young painter you are overwhelmed by the complexity of your subject. Every crease, every dimple, is an equally startling revelation. It's like your first girl. You don't understand her. You can only copy her – hesitantly. Later you become shamelessly yourself. You create in your image – as nearly life-size as possible.

When hundreds of gulls circle in the sky and the light is horizontal so that their black and white are merged together into silver, they look like a shoal of the herrings they live off. And so imagine the sea and sky to be interchangeable. Imagine turning them upside down like the globes of a sand hour-glass. Thus this painting.

Janos often prepared for his paintings by making etchings. He was a masterly printer. The press was in a dark alcove off one corner of the studio, so that even in daylight it was impossible to work there without having the light on. He wore an old overall of Diana's tied like an apron around his waist. As he stood there hunched over what he was doing with his hands, the light from the naked bulb shone on his bald patch and his sparse, dried, old man's hair. He wipes the ink off the plate, and between each wipe cleans his hand by rubbing it on the apron down his thighs. There is the bitter smell of the slightly warm ink and the mild fumes from the acid bath. The smell, the harsh light, the intent physical patience of the man, suggest a basement cobbler. And there is something of the artisan in his pride. After he has put the print through the press, he picks it up – with a piece of clean scrap-paper between his knobbly finger and thumb so as not to fingerprint it – glances at it, turns it towards me and says, ' That is the best you will get in any place.'

JANUARY 27

I have begun *The Waves* on the canvas. It wants three perspectives: the perspective of the sky, of the waves and of the underwater. But it shall have none. The colours by themselves must tug away like kites – like the little bits of coloured canvas they are. Yet these little bits of coloured canvas must convey all that Icarus fell through and into. What demon of purity is it that prevents me including Icarus himself in the picture? That man can now fly? That today we have a horror of the specific because our minds reach out for an ever larger and larger synthesis?

Because I am suspicious of stories in paint? I suspect none of these is the answer. Rather it is that the painter has become the unseen protagonist in his own paintings.

FEBRUARY 7

From the top of a bus I saw a head of hair so reminiscent of Yvonne that I turned round to look at the face beneath. So different. This was a typist's face with spectacles. Her hair was the colour of flax, the same colour as the lightest parts of her legs where they were sunburnt. Flaxen, I suppose, is the word. But what poor justice the conventional adjective does to the unexpected noun that I discovered just then with something of the delight with which twenty-five years ago I discovered her name. I read the paper over her shoulder in the Metro, till she looked up at me. She lived at Argenteuil. The first present I gave her was a bracelet. Michel had bought it for his Jeanne, who afterwards set her hat at me. They had a furious row, and Michel threw the bracelet out of the window into the courtyard. I was coming in and picked it up. 'Keep it,' Michel screamed when I handed it to him, 'give it to the flics – they can use it for a handcuff.' Michel was always unhappy in love. And despite his surrealist success he was an indifferent painter. But – he was reckless. That's what I liked about him. One day he had the idea of having a photograph taken of himself removing a swarm of bees – with nets and gloves and all the accoutrements. He had it done, and was in hospital for a week poisoned with the stings he had received. Now he is in the history-of-art books. Anyway, six months after I had given her the bracelet, Yvonne said, 'No one could love you. You are a political machine.' Diana has more than once used the same words. Which is odd, because I am certainly no political machine now. My politics are a lightning conductor. It is my way of life they have hated, my obstinacy.

This Michel, whose surname is well known, was later to play a brief but important part in Janos's life in London. Of Yvonne I know nothing.

Diana, Janos's wife, was forty-two but, although attractive, looked a little older. She had a well-formed body, with strong, elegant legs. It was her face which made her look older: the set mouth, the worried eyes. One had the impression of somebody who needed sunlight. One could imagine her, brown hair tousled, in trousers on a yacht. But she was pale, her hair was almost straight, and she looked as if she had lived for years doing dutiful social work in the heart of a city.

When she had married Janos at twenty-five, she must have had that quality of English upper-class girls which is accurately called flower-like, but derives, as even in Elizabethan poetry, from laid-out lawns and beds tended by a whole team of gardeners.

She met Janos in 1938. He had just arrived in England as a refugee, and she was working for one of the organizations for helping Jews and Nazi victims to get out of Germany. Previously she had been to Oxford, where she had found an intellectual basis for her revolt against her family. Spain, modern poetry and the Left Book Club as opposed to the Côte d'Azur, small-talk and week-end house parties. That is not to say her political ideas were insincere. She had wanted, like many others, a larger life; which in principle is a sound emancipating desire.

She married Janos within a few months of meeting him. To her, then, Janos must have stood as hero, victim, the large life and the European struggle, as well as a forty-year-old male. It is difficult to say what future she had visualized for them both. Perhaps she had not visualized very much: 1938 was not a year for long-term plans.

Yet somewhere in the back of her mind, she must have had vague expectations which had even contributed to her falling in love. Sex covers a multitude of hopes. I doubt whether she had ever thought of having children. All her maternal feelings were probably centred on Janos himself. Partly because he was an artist and the cultivated naïveté of artists often strikes women as though it were the same thing as the natural naïveté of children – a mistake which can lead to severe disillusionment because cultivated as opposed to natural naïveté does not develop, does not respond to maternal moulding. Partly because, quite simply, Janos was a refugee.

I write 'quite simply', but one must not over-simplify. On one level only was it simple. Janos, a foreigner, had arrived from the mainland of Europe, where a world war had been fought, the first Socialist revolution achieved and Fascism unleashed – arrived from this mainland, without money, friends or language, in London: the

23

most formal and secluded capital in Europe, where only the secret manipulators can act with uninhibited directness. Diana must have seen immediately how she could be Janos's interpreter, how to begin with she could finance him, and, above all, how she could be his guide, his contact with the necessary manipulators.

Yet it was here that Diana's expectations ceased to be simple, for she had no intention of turning Janos into an English gentleman. To do so would be to betray all that he could give her. She knew that her four or five years of revolt had not really destroyed her past or superimposed itself on her upbringing. Now, however, with Janos she could turn her advantages and privileges to some purpose: a purpose which exactly coincided with her revolt against those same advantages and privileges. Janos could rescue her by allowing her to help him.

She had never been hungry. She had never been interrogated. She had never been smuggled over a frontier. She had sat in committee-rooms. She had shouted in Trafalgar Square. She had been to the Welsh valleys to see the beginning of the marches. But the way she had arrived at doing such things always remained there as a possible way of retreat. She had never been cut-off. Whereas Janos was entirely cut-off. His voice, that had whispered a warning to a companion as he had jumped off a tram before his destination to deceive a suspected pursuer, called her Rosie. His eyes that had read clandestine documents looked at her with the same intentness. His hands that had been clenched to keep himself desperately steady, caressed her into delicious unsteadiness. He seldom talked of his personal experiences. But it was unnecessary to her for him to do so. They were now part of his very sex that had survived them. If Janos married her, she would be included in all that his exile meant. And then, exiled with him, she would be able to fight for them both in the country where her privileged birth gave her certain advantages, which as exiles they would certainly need.

Janos had already been married once, to Kati. They had met as students and she had become a cabaret singer. From Janos's photograph of her she looked like a gypsy: proud and fated; a lean face; daring, frantic eyes; a mouth like an orchid, and a mane of black hair. 'On the stage,' he used to say, 'with the lights on her face, she was like some animal caught in the lights of a car. Mein Kaninchen. Yes. But she was always trapped.' Two years after they were married, she was taken to an asylum, and later it was reported that she had killed herself.

How different Diana must have appeared to him. She also was nervous. But she would have been called slim, not lean. In the difference between those two words lay a little of the difference between the Europe from which Janos had fled and the English garden Diana had walked out of. I imagine that it was Diana's simplicity that struck him. She was, in fact, a highly complex character; but she had witnessed and experienced little that was fatal, and the fatal complicates as does nothing else.

I can picture Diana working in the refugee relief office, austerely efficient. There is no time to be lost, no time for frivolity, but just because there usually is frivolity in the storm-centre itself, her earnestness is unlike any Janos has ever seen. She scowls at the news, but her complexion is like an early summer morning on which everything is shot, like silk, with well-being. She says they must get the Spanish Republicans out of the French concentration camps, but she speaks as if that in itself would be a glorious victory. When Janos gives her a sketch-book of drawings, she clasps it to her breast like a brooch and cries, 'How lovely!' before she has turned one page. When he asks her out to supper, she says she couldn't possibly because every evening she must write their Fund letters. As in the life of a fortunate child, everything has its appointed place. But she is, after all, not a child. Her breasts press against the printed flowers on her dress. Her always clean arms are white. Her innocent sense of order, unlike a child's, promises security. Her nakedness assures safety.

The Channel is the Rubicon for a European refugee, wider perhaps than the Atlantic. Having crossed it, Janos looks back on the last twenty-five years of his life. He sees his own past experiences pursuing him like a pack of wild animals, and he sees Diana standing as safe as her namesake.

She stands, it seems to him, sentinel at either end of a phase of his life; and so, marking off that phase — those twenty-five years — she gives it meaning. She represents his childhood, not because she has anything in common with it, but because she has not known any of the things which separate him from it. She reminds him of it, as it were, by omission. And at the same time she is standing beside him now in a country where he will live openly, normally again. He will

25

fight in the coming war, about which he has no illusions. Yet in a sense that war already belongs to the past – he has been fighting it for twenty years. Deeper than anything else in his mind is his conviction that he must in the future work – paint – unceasingly. But for a painter to work, he needs – probably more than any other kind of artist – a sense of permanence. Diana embodies such a sense of permanence, and he, by protecting its innocence with his experience, will share in it.

To put it very simply, I believe that Janos fell in love with Diana rather as, after years in a city, a man can fall in love with a mountain village and decide to build a cabin there; but, as I have said, Diana fell in love with Janos to become a scheming exile, and to overthrow, in her own way, the capital.

FEBRUARY 22

Red like radishes when you wash them under a tap and then open your hand to see if they are clean.

Red, brick red, like a girl's nipples in love.

The same red as the hills of Calabria.

Red like the hands of a woman scrubbing.

Red like a paprika.

Red like nothing: red that is simply a colour on a canvas.

Red that has as many layers of meaning as there are red objects in the world.

There is no red in *The Waves*. I must wait for another canvas.

MARCH 9

Now that it is spring I have taken to getting up half an hour earlier and going for a short walk before work. I still, in general, hate London. But I have my favourite areas – the Edgware Road, Woolwich and of course Hampstead Heath. In these places I know what I am meant to be doing.

In fact, Janos walked a lot, far more than the average Londoner. In all weathers he wore his beret. But he was punctilious about changing his jacket or even his trousers, if they were paint-spotted, before going out. Whilst walking he had, like most painters, an eye whose fancy one could not predict. An unusually white wall,

a pile of chairs on the sidewalk, a negress – these he might pick out
whilst ignoring a magnolia tree in full bloom.

MARCH 12

The Waves progresses. It is odd that I am so fascinated by the
sea, which I never saw for the first twenty years of my life.
But a sky above a sea is often very like the sky above the Alföld.
Writing which suddenly reminds me of a dream I had last
night. I was on my uncle's farm where I used to go as a boy
during the harvesting. We were outside the cottage, and my
aunt had set up a trestle table with food on it. Several friends
were there, and our chickens were pecking round the hooves of
their horses. On to the huge Alföld sky a film was being
projected as if it were a screen – a film of incidents from my life
and of my paintings. I remember distinctly that it was in colour.
At the end of the film, everyone was wildly enthusiastic. 'Wonderful,' they shouted, 'wonderful!' And my mother, who in my
dream was as old as the last time I saw her in 1920, was so
pleased and so proud that she began pouring out wine for the
whole crowd. But I took her to one side and, bending down to
her ear beneath her plaited grey hair, I whispered, 'Keep the
wine. You will need it for yourself. It is only the Délibáb they
are applauding.'

... The Délibáb is a sky mirage that appears over the Hungarian
plain. In the sky, just above the horizon, one sees the upside down
image of a church tower that is actually invisible on the far side of
the horizon. •

MARCH 14

Yesterday I took a day off which ended badly. The painter
should never stop painting. John arranged for me to go down
with him to see Sir Gerald Banks's collection. Perhaps I was
more tired and strained than I realized, as a result of the last few
weeks. Anyway, I lost my temper with Banks's, wasted energy,
infuriated poor Diana when I told her about it, and left myself
in no state to work today.

The whole of this day is still vivid in my memory.
Sir Gerald Banks had invited me down to his country house to

see his private collection. I had asked if I might bring *Janos*, a painter friend of mine, and Banks had agreed. At the small country station in Oxfordshire our host was waiting for us on the platform. As usual, *Janos* bowed slightly at the introduction.

'Did you have a good journey?' His manner was distant but formally welcoming. He behaved as though the railway-station was his front door. We followed him out to his Bentley, in which both of us sat in the back like diplomats.

'What kind of car is this?' asked *Janos*.

Sir Gerald explained, adding, 'My son's always telling me it's old-fashioned to drive a Bentley nowadays. But in their way they're works of art.' He sounded the horn as we overtook a van. 'To drive one is a kind of aesthetic experience, you know.' He smiled into the driving-mirror; his features in his over-size square head were small, so his face was not dramatically changed by any expression; his smile was most noticeable in the relaxing of his jaw. 'Naturally it's an aesthetic experience of a low order. But I'd rather have a Bentley than, say, a Greuze.'

'Do you ski?' asked *Janos*.

'No. I never have.'

'If you collect experiences – that is one to prize.'

I made some remark about the view.

'Landscape begins about here.'

'How long have you been here?'

'Only about eighteen months. My wife came down to see some friends at Oxford, happened to drive out this way, saw the house – and telephoned me that night. It had been empty for years. It was a fifteenth-century monastery originally.'

We entered through two large white gates.

'There's a pretty little stream down there' – Sir Gerald pointed down the hill on the left – 'where we have magnificent kingcups in the spring.'

'Kingcups. They are a kind of what?' asked *Janos*.

'A kind of extra large regal buttercup.'

As we stepped out of the car, two boxer dogs bounded down the wide steps from the front porch. The house winged itself away on either side. The chimney-stacks, ranging from Elizabethan to nineteenth century, gave the impression of a whole village clustered behind.

Lady Banks had fair hair gathered up on the top of her head. She was a woman of about forty-five. The lower part of her face was very sharply formed, but her eyes were thin and nervous.

'I'm delighted you've come,' she said, taking my hand. 'I've wanted to meet you for a long time. You have an individual point of view – and that's what most people lack these days.'

'He has not a point of view. He has a philosophical system,' interrupted Janos.

She turned round abruptly. Janos extended his hand, smiled and said, 'Janos Lavin.'

'So you're the painter. I do hope I'll have a chance of seeing some of your work some time. I wanted my husband to ask you to bring some down, but he said you couldn't do that sort of thing.'

'I'm sure you'd like a drink,' said Sir Gerald.

Inside, the house had a curious atmosphere which at first was difficult to pin down. Actually it was an historical atmosphere – though not in the usual guide-book sense of the term. It was the result of three very different modes of living being superimposed one on top of another. The bare stones of the wide corridors, the mullioned windows lining the long rooms, the wooden roofs, these belonged to the original monastic period. But the cloak-room where we left our coats, the willow-pattern lavatory pan, the large doors with black knobs, belonged to a rambling country house as it still might be lived in today. Then finally, dominating both these previous modes, there was what the Banks' had brought with them: the fine 18th-century furniture of an urban house – a house, say, in Regent's Park – modern-framed pictures, a Tang horse, and that special air of being in European demand which goes with embassy invitations on the mantelpiece.

Lady Banks conducted us into a room where a large fire was burning. Down the centre of the room was a long table with new Italian, Swiss, German, American art books laid out on it – as in a public library during an art festival. On the walls were two Gauguins, a Michelangelo drawing and a large Degas pastel of a nude. We stood by the fireplace and made the usual kindling remarks.

Soon Janos walked across to examine the Degas, stepped back from it, frowned in admiration, almost pressed his nose to the glass again, and then, coming back towards us, waved over his shoulder towards the picture.

'*That — it is formidable, magnificent.*'

'*It's not really one of my favourites,*' said Lady Banks in an emphatic voice; '*although it is often admired. Who was it the other week, Jerry, who went on and on about it? Oh yes. Nigel — he said he'd write a story about it.*'

Banks turned towards Janos. '*You're right, of course. It is magnificent, and one of the few pastels, I feel, that has as much tension, as much ruthlessness, as the bronzes.*'

The word '*ruthlessness*' was obviously difficult to say.

'*Do sit down,*' chimed our hostess. We settled.

Lunch was highly formalized. I sat opposite Janos and a Cézanne, with Lady Banks on my left and Sir Gerald on my right. The dishes and the maid's attentions divided the conversation into small speeches.

It was like an official private interview in an embassy which, for sound diplomatic reasons, must not go beyond a certain point in discussion, duration and familiarity.

During coffee the speeches became longer. Janos leaned forward with his elbows on the table and played with the cruet. Lady Banks leaned back a little in her chair, smoked a cigarette and watched her husband like a trainer; whilst Sir Gerald filled out his ambassadorial rôle. His small, intelligent eyes in a square head visualized every problem in its proper perspective. He told us about the warring factions in his province, the difficulties to be met with in local prejudice, the broad outline of the world plan; he confessed that occasionally for diplomatic reasons he had to take steps which he would rather not have to take; he gave us to believe that soon he might be transferred so that his accumulated experience might be applied in a broader context; and, throughout, his view was the large one, larger than that of the protagonists themselves, for whom nevertheless he had the greatest respect. I remember him ending one statement, his hands palm down on the table and his arms outstretched in front of him, by saying, '*After all, we must admit that more often than not genius is blind to its own achievements.*'

When we had finished our cigars, Lady Banks left us and we began the tour of the house. It was for this that we had been invited. The collection was certainly impressive, but not because it had been acquired with anything so vulgar as untold wealth. It was impressive because it reflected the discerning, intelligent, catholic taste of a man who had a wide knowledge of European art and enough money to buy about a quarter of what he wanted.

At first both Janos and I looked eagerly at each work. It was a little like being shown round a rare garden: Sir Gerald standing in his pale grey suit beside each plant and knowing everything about it according to the catalogues; Janos, an expert practical gardener, bending foward, fingering the light with one hand and absent-mindedly scratching his leg with the other.

'The purist phase of Cubism,' Banks said of a Picasso.

A boxer dog ran into the room, and then, seeing us, pulled up short and slid on one of the Persian carpets over the parquet.

'Out, Tilly! Kitchen! Kitchen! Tilly!'

We proceeded from carpet to carpet and from room to room.

But after a while I could see that Janos was growing either impatient or bored. He left me to reply to Sir Gerald's remarks, and instead of concentrating on the pictures (which in themselves were at least as interesting as those with which we had begun the tour) he began looking vaguely round – at the carpets, the ceiling, the skirting-boards. His hands, which, when he was involved and interested in something, were always fingering the air for words as though they were working glove puppets to illustrate his ideas, were now in his trouser pockets. If there was just something of the official guide about Sir Gerald, there was now certainly something of the bored member of the public at the back of the conducted crowd about Janos.

We mounted a fine staircase. From a window half-way up it we looked down on a geometric rose garden below.

'The monastery garden,' said Sir Gerald with an ironic smile. 'I've thought, you know, about turning the whole place into a country museum, with a faculty for students attached. It would be an ideal setting, don't you think?'

We descended another staircase, Janos looking more morose than ever, and entered a room with french windows at one end and a lawn outside. The light was turning gold before it disappeared. It was a feminine-looking room, and we went up to study the Fragonard and Watteau drawings on the wall. Banks put his hand to a Watteau red conté drawing and sucked in his breath with admiration. Something about it must have particularly interested Janos,

31

for he craned forward to examine it – momentarily and suddenly interested again.

'I'm glad you like it,' said Banks in a confiding way. 'It's one of the small things I value most in the whole house. It's a beautiful drawing in its own right – who else but Watteau could draw a silk coat suggesting the very warmth it gathers from the body, yet also prophesying that soon it will lie forsaken across a chair? Its mortal secret has been whispered on to the paper, and yet its form is as clear, as clear in its own way as Piero's.' He was no longer confiding: he was now lecturing. 'But I also value this drawing because it seems to me to suggest a certain attitude to art, to life. Not its subject, of course. That is so much aristocratic playing – vieux jeu in the most accurate sense. No, what it affirms so poignantly is what I call the unlikeliness of art.' Banks had now turned completely away from the drawing, but looked at us only occasionally; his eyes scanned the room and constantly rested on the door as though he were expecting another more important visitor to join his audience. 'Art begins, if the wind is right and the sails are properly trimmed, at that point where we forget our destination and the purpose of our voyage – art begins when we can dare to be detached – both painter and viewer! True art is only born of risk – the risk of yielding to extreme irresponsibility in the midst of a life compelling us to accept one more responsibility after another. This is why Plato considered the artist a menace. And he is a menace, my God! Yet occasionally a work escapes his own self-destruction, and escapes the counter measures that the world is forced to take against him, and occasionally the work then turns out to be a masterpiece – to be a drawing like this. Look at it. The frail imprint on this small browned piece of paper that has miraculously escaped the artist, the counter measures, the dustpan of the woman tidying up, the ravages of four major European wars. It has escaped all these, and then – I find it amongst the wastepaper of the galleries, amongst the thousands of drawings done by men who have never risked anything. And in order to save it, I too must be irresponsible, for I must stoop to pick it up, whilst everyone else runs on. Who knows how long it will be before another man feels that he can risk anything for this small scrap of paper?'

Sir Gerald shrugged his shoulders to express that kind of uncertainty which is lined with pleasure.

Janos was scowling, looking at the floor, refusing to meet Sir Gerald's eyes. I thought he would turn away to look at another picture. But suddenly he raised his head, and said, very flatly, as though it were a duty he didn't fully admit having to perform. 'I do not understand. You bent down to pick this up. Now it is up. Why must you have more risks?'

Banks seemed unaware of how he had provoked his listener. He merely thought he had been misunderstood. He suffered fools gladly because to him all seemed fools. Patiently he began to explain to the imaginary lecture hall.

'To look at it is a risk. To look at it properly and fully is to sever – even if only momentarily – one's obligations, to forget one's ambitions, to contemplate for one moment with Watteau without the slightest consideration of expediency. And after having severed and forgotten, there is the grave risk that one will never be able to find one's way back to the original spot. In this the seduction of art is like every other kind of seduction. We're all of us, all of us who are connected with art, slaves to a divine trollop.'

Janos no longer looked at the floor. He had corrected his normal stoop, and was upright, his eyes focused six inches in front of him as though he had already seized Banks by the lapels and was staring into his face.

'That is cloudy merde *nonsense,' he said in a voice several tones deeper than usual.*

'I beg your pardon?' said Banks, who had heard perfectly.

'There is no risk – never – here.' Janos waved up at the ceiling.

Banks realized that he had been misunderstood again. The man was obtuse.

'But, my dear –'

'Surely –' I began. But it was too late. The whole of Janos's body was now drawn tight with anger. He glared at Banks, his eyes like the hitting ends of two hammers. Banks just perceptibly drew back his square head so that the back of it was in a straight line with his shoulder-blades. Janos strode across the room towards the table by the window. Sir Gerald went relaxed, and watched him with consciously, ironically raised eyebrows. Janos seized a majolica pot which was on the table, and swivelled round with it in his hand.

'Regard this bucket,' he shouted – his vocabulary had become as wild as his gestures. 'Drop your eyes in it. A man did it. Made it – I

33

mean. *He made thousands. Like sighs. Lots a day. There was more risks, more pain, more hurted hands, more tired eyes, more risks I tell you, in this potman making one day than you for all your life!'*

Banks waited for more. But Janos had finished. He turned back and put the pot on the table. His hands were shaking. As he did so, one of the boxer dogs came through the curtains that halved the large room. Janos turned round towards the sudden movement. His arm caught the pot, and it fell to the floor. It smashed into many pieces. The dog retreated, startled. One piece of the pot, larger than the others, continued to rock on its curved side. All the other pieces were motionless fragments. Janos didn't give one glance at the floor, but immediately looked round and stared at Banks. Banks shook his head and smiled. Janos continued to stare at him in accusation.

If a stranger had entered the room at that moment and could have instantly summed up the apparent situation, he would have concluded that Banks had just broken one of Janos's most treasured possessions.

'*Of no account at all. I assure you. It doesn't matter at all,*' he said at last and called to the dog that was standing motionless by the curtain. '*Tilly, come here.*' Then striding across to the door and opening it, he shouted, '*Come on – out, Tilly!*'

He banged the door behind the dog, fingered his tie, and went across to Janos, who was standing with his hands in his pockets by the pieces of the jug.

'*You misunderstood me, Mr Lavin. No – don't apologize. It doesn't matter at all. It is a good lesson for a collector. And perhaps it even proves my point – about the fragility of art. No?*'

He laughed, put his hand on Janos's arm and led him through the curtain.

'*Do you admire Hokusai, Mr Lavin?*'

Janos had not yet said a word. Now he spoke very quietly.

'*We must go, John.*'

'*My dear fellow, of course you mustn't. I have lots more to show you. Do please forget about it. And, anyway, it was certainly not your fault. It's what happens when the dogs have the run of the house.*'

And again he took Janos's arm and led him up to six Hokusai prints. The tour continued. But now Janos gave – or pretended to

34

give – all his attention to the pictures. And Banks gave all his attention to Janos. Nor was this, I believe, merely a question of politeness or etiquette. Janos had suddenly taken the place of the important visitor who might have arrived. At one moment Banks caught my eye, and glancing at Janos's back, smiled at me. He had lost one majolica pot from his collection, but he had gained a character, a man of strangely intense and erratic passion.

As we went down one of the dark-panelled corridors to a further room, Janos stopped me, and, jerking his head to indicate the direction we had come from, whispered:

'We must go.'

'It's all right,' I said. 'What's one pot to him?'

'That's not the question,' he muttered severely.

'We've got to wait for him to take us to the station.'

'Have you lost your way?' Sir Gerald's host-voice came out of the dark.

'Then I shall speak to him,' Janos said. He was already walking down the corridor ahead of me. The room at the end was a large rectangular library. Books lined each of the long walls. The roof was a wooden one with bare beams. At the far end of the room was a writing-table on which Sir Gerald was sitting, dangling one leg. Janos stopped several yards away from him in the middle of the empty floor. There was a strong lamp on the writing-table, but otherwise the room was only dimly lit with wall brackets, and one could see the brown silhouettes of big trees through the window.

'Sir Gerald Banks!' Janos's voice was calm but insistent, and there was a slight echo in the room. He stood where he was, an unreasonable distance away from Banks, as if it were impossible for him to take another step forward, like a man standing in the bow of his boat calling to a figure on the quayside. Banks stopped swinging his leg.

'I owe you an apology.'

'My dear Lavin, I've told you –'

'I do not speak of breaking your pot. I lost my temper. But after losing your temper you must make reconciliation or you must go. I was not making reconciliation because I was unable. But neither did I go. That is from where I owe you an apology.'

Banks was obviously interested. I imagined him thinking – the extraordinary formality of the elderly foreigner! How near they are

to the whole formalized etiquette of insults, provocations and duels!
Janos still stood on the same spot.

'Tell me one thing,' said Banks in an easy conversational tone
that implied that surely the whole thing, apologies and all, was over
now, 'what is it that you disapproved of so much?'

'You want an honest answer?' Janos hesitated, not because he
was going to stop but because he wanted to mark the beginning of
what he had to say. 'This. All this,' he added.

'But that is what you came to see.'

'I was coming to see some paintings.'

'The collection mostly is of paintings'

'Flowers look different in different button-holes.'

Banks did not flinch at the insult. On the contrary, he smiled. He
wanted to possess the whole situation and all that might result from
it. Janos, still standing on the same spot, was also relaxed now, with
one hand in his jacket pocket.

'Tell me what is so shocking about mine?'

'This house, it is like the house of a man who shoots in the
jungle.'

'A big game hunter?' Sir Gerald laughed. The writing-lamp
illuminated his confident face. He was lit like a character in the
centre of the stage, whilst Janos, in the dim light, spoke like a man
from the wings.

'That is right. It is the collection of a big game hunter. All these
works in your house were alive once. Now they seem dead. And do
not misunderstand me. I respect your skill. You understood them.
You faced them. You won them. You are an expert – one of the
few. You understand the artistic animal. But now on the walls,
with little titles on silver plates beneath them, all these prizes –
trophies – they celebrate your skill, not their own wild life. But it is
not so good as a big game hunter. Because the artistic hunt is not
dangerous.'

'But surely all private collections are like that. If you possess a
work of art and you believe it to be good, you cannot avoid being
proud of it. Even the Renaissance princes had the same attitude. I
can't see that a little reflected glory is such a terrible thing. You're
an idealist, Lavin.' He said the word idealist as all men of the
world do – with affection.

'No, you are wrong. I am a painter, not the idealist. Do you

know who artists paint for? I will tell you. They paint for heroes.'
The emphasis with which Janos was speaking contrasted oddly with
his tired, leathery face and his old man's bald patches and hair.

'Even today?'

'Even today. Today artists paint for themselves. They are cut off,
and so they have become their own heroes. In the Renaissance the
princes were the new heroes. In the eighteenth century the middle-
class merchant who wanted pictures of horses and his wife – even he
was a kind of hero, too.'

'Well!' said Banks benignly.

'Today, look. The collector, he is no hero. That is why you' –
Janos put his hand towards Banks – 'you have to pretend and make
fairy-tales about the risk in looking at the work of art. The modern
collector, he cannot deserve the reflected glory. He is no hero. I ask
you. Do you think Picasso paints for rich apartments?'

'He sells his work to whoever can afford it.'

'Of course. He cannot make heroes like he can make pictures. I
ask you. Do you think Gonzalez beat the iron to make the ornament
for the rose garden?'

'Most of Gonzalez' sculptures are in museums.'

'We put modern works into museums for the same exact reason
as we put the old works in. The old heroes are dead. And the new
ones, they do not exist.'

'All right. I disagree profoundly – but tell me one thing. If you
disapprove of all private collectors and all museums, what do you
believe in? How are artists to live?'

'I do not disapprove. I become impatient.'

'But in the meanwhile, my dear fellow. In the meanwhile, you
have to live. Maybe the private patron of today isn't a Medici.'

'Why do you never commission anything?'

'I believe the artist works better if he has complete freedom. We
have learnt that now.'

'You think so? You do not think it is because you know you
cannot inspire him? Because you know you do not share ideas with
him. Except ideas about form. You do not commission him because
you have no subjects. The artist is unemployable – that is why he is
free. No one really knows what he should be used for. And so he
makes exercises, he makes pure colours and pure shapes – the
abstract art – until it has been decided what he can do. But do the

collectors help to decide? They cannot. I will tell you. Once the patron was like a man with a hawk on his wrist to hunt the truth for him. Now he is like an old lady who keeps canaries.'

Banks laughed at this. Then he said:

'No private patrons, no museums. You are left with state art.'

'Yes.'

'But what of the appalling dangers of that – made a hundred times worse if it is a monopoly? You can't really believe in committee art. The taste of the lowest common denominator.'

'In state art there are real dangers. But I prefer them to the ones you have to invent.' Janos's voice was rising again.

'The ones I invent?'

'Your risk which you say happens when you look at a picture.'

'Oh, but that was a manner of speaking. It's not what we're talking about now at all. I ask you – look at Russia.'

'And that is a manner of doing. Sometimes it is terrible. But you, you can make no mistakes. That is your trouble.'

'Mistakes? Surely you don't –'

At this moment Lady Banks entered the room. When he saw her, Sir Gerald stopped talking.

'There you are!' she said.

It was immediately clear from her voice that she was angry. It had the metallic ring of polite hostess-anger. She must have heard about the accident, and it appeared that she held all three of us responsible.

'In the dark!' she added.

Back in front of the fire, Lady Banks asked her husband if he were going to take us to the station or should she. Visiting hours were over.

'Did you enjoy the collection, Mr Lavin?'

Before Janos could reply, Banks said:

'He had very interesting objections to the principles involved.'

'Apparently.' She turned sharply away. Her hair at the back was swept tightly up through a comb; not a strand was loose.

Banks handed Janos a whisky.

'You must come and see my contemporary pictures in London some time.'

We talked for ten minutes awkwardly. The only one of us who was completely assured was Lady Banks. She knew what she

38

wanted – an apology. She kept leading the conversation back to the afternoon's tour and the collection, staring hard and aggressively at Janos. Sir Gerald is a man who is never obviously ill at ease, and he had resumed his formal ambassadorial manner. Yet, if in the arc of light at the end of the bare library he had seemed, throughout that unusually pointed conversation, to be the main character on a stage, he now behaved like an eminent member of the audience leaving his box after the abrupt but final curtain. The romantic diversion was over. One was back with one's wife, one's responsibilities, the need to find a taxi.

As for Janos, he was waiting to go.

We got up. Lady Banks held out her hand.

'And next time, Mr Lavin, I do hope I'll have seen some of your works – somewhere.'

We said good-bye to Sir Gerald Banks outside the station. His large face, which seemed even larger in the dim light, was like a prime minister's on an election poster, and he wore his coat like a toga.

'I must say,' he said, looking through the rain on to the wet railway lines the other side of the fence, 'I envy you going your separate ways tonight into that endless city.'

John thought it admirable that I told Banks what I thought of him. But in fact he misunderstood the situation. I did not decide to behave as I did. I did not act according to a principle. I reacted. What I did was like a reflex action. Most protests are like that. You can put your principles into a match-box, but what fills the whole room are your instinctive responses, the consequences of your past experience. In this case I should have controlled them. I did nothing except betray myself. *The Waves* look terrible.

MARCH 18

I worked badly today, and consequently, as so often, I quarrelled with Diana. She came in from that damned library tired and washed out. 'A good day?' she asked, because hers had been a bad one like mine. 'No,' I replied, and she sighed and went to have a bath in that bathroom she thinks is not fit to pluck chickens in. Later we went for a silent walk together, and I suddenly realized that the gulls should be light against dark, not – as in the etching which misled me – dark against light.

Diana had a very small private income, about £200 a year, which she supplemented by part-time work at the Municipal Library.

MARCH 23

When I get stuck in the middle of a work, the difficulty, the delay, is always the result of an earlier mistake I have made without realizing it. I now have to climb over the obstacle that blocks my path. But the point of my climbing it is that when at last I get on top and sit astride it, I can see the path I should have taken to avoid the obstacle altogether. Then I climb down, go back and take the proper path. I do not overcome the obstacle – even though I have proved that I can by climbing over it. A work of art is not the result of a series of conquests. If it were, the first-year student would be a genius for he has more conquests to his name. It is the result of something far more difficult – of finding a direct, logical, firm route through a landscape cluttered with every conceivable kind of boulder, barrier and obstacle. The artist should make a maze seem a highway.

The Waves are still a maze.

MARCH 25

I cannot pass Trafalgar Square with its pigeons without thinking of Laszlo and his poem. It is surprising that I think of the poem first, and only afterwards of the actual pigeons and the actual incident at Kecskemét. I don't think I have ever laughed since as I laughed with Laci. We laughed at everything that would now seem frustrating and hypocritical because we were so certain we could do away with it. We laughed – in a different way – at everything that would now seem determined and noble, because we took such qualities for granted.

From recent photographs of him, addressing the Writers' Union in Budapest or pronouncing upon the New Literature, I have the impression that he laughs less now. There is still the same upper lip which could never lie quite still on the lower.

But the face has been closed somewhat by responsibility. I wonder if he remembers as clearly as I do how we talked of the Fourth Man – for whom he now is so responsible. There were three of us, Laszlo, Ernö and myself – a poet, an architect and a painter. In turn each of us would find ourselves broke, disheartened or getting stupidly violent. Then this one would turn to the other two for support – which they would anticipate. Once Laci said we were like three men holding a sheet, always encouraging each other to keep it taut because we were waiting for a fourth man to jump down from the sky – into the sheet.

Ernö is dead. I am here. Only Laszlo saw that fourth, Socialist man appear. And so he bears heavy responsibilities.

In what way do those responsibilities now force him to think of me? He cannot of course see the work I'm doing – or will still do. Yet if he could, would it make any difference? How much benefit of doubt have twenty years of devoted political involvement earned me? Possibly none. The fact of a generation ageing should not be allowed to impair the vigilance of the defence of Socialism. I have not returned to contribute. And this fact must affect all my judgements. I admire Laszlo for becoming more of an administrator and less of a poet. But despite my admiration, he may not have done that at all. That may well be a spectator's distinction.

I wonder if he is married. That is not the kind of fact one reads about him.

The most critical decision of my life, though at the time it was casual enough, was when I decided to come west instead of going to Moscow. And the reason behind my decision now seems not only naïve but ironic. I wanted to go where I would still have to fight for Socialism. I did not want to enjoy the victory that others had fought for. Yet it is Laci who still fights.

Janos seldom talked to me about Laszlo; and after his death, never. Even at this time, I had the impression that for Janos to talk about him was to bare some old wound. He did, however, tell me of the poem about the Kecskemét pigeons.

During the Soviet Government of 1919, small bands of reactionaries, who were later to become the famous White Terrorists, occasionally attacked well-known Socialists or Socialist meetings.

Janos and Laszlo were in the small town of Kecskemét when one of these attacks took place. The White Terrorists had hidden themselves in a school overlooking the square where a public meeting was being held. The pigeons in the square, accustomed to being fed from the school windows, flew up to the sills when they saw a number of figures appear there. A few moments later, when these figures shot at the speakers addressing the meeting (killing one), the pigeons scattered into the sky and circled high above the town, whilst the crowd ran in all directions to seek cover. Later Laszlo wrote his poem about this incident and compared the birds that rose above the shots to the spirit of the people. 'But,' added Janos, 'during the real Terror, the pigeons were back in the square, peaceful as ever. Which proves that the best fighting image for man is man. No?'

MARCH 28

I have reached another impasse with *The Waves*. And so I drew all day instead. On such days, when I have temporarily abandoned the major painting, if I do not draw, my mind becomes overcrowded, and the crowd accuses.

Usually company restores my faith in myself, and I was delighted when Len Hancock and his wife dropped in for some coffee after supper. Diana was hemming some sheets, silently and dutifully. When I am depressed, her worst fears are confirmed. We sit here at the bottom of the full studio – like lost souls to whom nothing can ever happen again. 'Everything,' I can almost hear her thinking, 'passes us by, and these sheets are disgraceful.' When I am not depressed my confidence supports her a little. Then she can at least become angry at what that confidence is directed towards. However, the Hancocks did not pass us by. And even Diana, who says she finds Len a bore, appeared pleased to see them.

He is an extraordinary man, Hancock: he is completely unharmed. Nothing has tarnished for him. He wants to make money to enjoy himself, and he does. He wants to worship his wife as a mannequin, and she asks for nothing better. He paints for pure pleasure, and painting gives it to him. Only aesthetes, political prudes or those, like poor Diana, who no longer believe in happiness, could disapprove of him.

Janos had got to know Len Hancock when meat was still rationed. There were already three butchers in the nearest shopping street, but this did not prevent Len starting a fourth. He bought the shop, had a new glass and chromium front put on it, and then piled the window with faggots, sausages, salamis, chicken fricassees, gulls' eggs, occasional cuts of venison and indeed anything that was un-rationed. Between the foods he arranged the flowers of the season. I have seen a split pig's head flanked by white roses, and plates of liver surrounded by daffodils! One afternoon when Janos and I were walking back to the studio, we went into this new shop to get some mincemeat.

At first sight, Hancock appeared oddly out of character with his surroundings. Immensely tall in his white jacket and apron, and with dark short-sighted eyes behind steel-rimmed spectacles, he looked more like an eccentric chemist than a cut-price shopkeeper. Only the speed, suggesting sleight of hand, with which he weighed and wrapped the mincemeat, revealed the sharper side of his character.

' You're an artist, aren't you?' he said, as Janos was counting out the money from his purse.

' Yes, I am,' replied Janos.

' I do a bit myself,' Hancock jerked his head to indicate the back of the shop, and then adjusted his metal spectacles with a large-thumbed, blood-stained hand.

' How do you know?' asked Janos, stuffing the meat into his coat pocket.

' Guessed it from your missus.'

We laughed, but Janos a little uncertainly.

' What do you go in for?'

' Sorry. I do not quite understand.'

' Well – landscapes, portraits – or are you one of these modern blokes?'

' Oh, I see. I paint' – Janos was still somewhat embarrassed and he shrugged his shoulders beneath his huge coat – 'many things.'

Hancock leaned across the counter, one hand on the scales, the needle of which banged up to the maximum. His head was still higher than ours.

' Do you have models?'

' Sometimes, yes.'

43

'*Lucky man! I'd give anything to have a go at a nude. But the wife won't have it.*'

'*No?*'

The next thing I heard about Hancock was the story of the cakes. There is a factory behind the Fulham Road which employs about a hundred girls, who like to buy cakes for their eleven-o'clock break. So one morning Hancock arranged in his window, beside the joints, the salamis and the flowers, a large tray of brightly coloured cakes – cakes whose colours vied with the plumage of tropical birds. Thus the cake trade began. But because even Hancock saw – if not from an aesthetic point of view, at least from a practical one – that you couldn't continue to mix up sugar cakes and kidneys, he had a separate counter put in at the back of the shop. Serving the cakes at this counter was, according to Janos, a most beautiful thirty-year-old woman. '*As beautiful as an Arab.*' And according to Diana, this was Hancock's wife.

Not long after, Hancock stopped Janos in the street. He was driving his van and, pulling up beside him, he asked Janos if he would like to see some of his pictures. There, tucked behind the meat deliveries, were two canvases. '*One landscape,*' said Janos, '*and one picture of wild ducks in the sky. They were brilliant and they were terrible. As clever, they were, as his shopkeeping, and as sweet as his cakes.*' As a result of this meeting, however, Janos asked Hancock and his wife to come round to the studio, and I was there the first evening they came.

Mrs Hancock was certainly beautiful. A slim athletic body and falling, long fair hair.

'*A real studio!*' she exclaimed as she came in. '*That's what Len's always going on about.*' Her voice had behind it a friendly Midland accent.

Her husband beamed over his glasses and squeezed her arm with his large red hand. '*Don't say that, Vee, or they'll think I'm just about to buy 'em out.*'

We sat and chatted and drank wine. Len told us his father had been a picture restorer, and that's how he had picked up the technique of painting.

'*One fine day I'll show you my copy of Rembrandt's* Slaughtered Ox. *There's light effects for you. A winner. I'd like to hang that one outside the shop, like they used to in the olden days. But* then all that yellow fat – it would put the customers right off.'

Mrs Hancock tasted the wine Janos had poured out for her.

'It's just like that wine we had in Brittany. Just like it, isn't it, Len?'

'It is a bit.'

'You like Brittany?'

'Like it? Once a year we're free. We pack up and we forget everything. A paint-box and easel in the back of the car for me. A swimming-suit for Vee. We stop where we like, and we stay for as long as we like. I paint and Vee sunbathes. La vie Bohème with a vengeance! Off into the wild!'

Mrs Hancock smiled, delighted.

Then Len suddenly asked, 'Could we see some of your pictures?'

Janos took half a dozen canvases from a pile, put one on the easel and stepped back to quiz it.

'Come and look, Vee.'

Hancock and his wife stared at the painting; he, wriggling his face like a dog its nose, and trying to imagine painting every square inch of it himself, and she, putting her head on one side and wondering. The painting was of an oncoming cyclist.

'It's a winner. Ah, you must have worked hard on that one, Mr Lavin.'

'It's certainly got a real life-like effect of speed,' added Mrs Hancock.

'Have you ever seen the bicycle race in France or Italy?' asked Janos. 'It is wonderful. The bicycle – herself the most beautiful machine we have made. And the crowds joining in. When it is very hot and the cyclists go through a village, all the girls get bottles of cold water, and as the boy cyclists go past, they throw the water over them to make them more cool. It is beautiful – that. No?'

'Yes, I can just imagine,' said Mrs Hancock, now put at her ease by this explanation. But her husband continued to peer at the painting, and eventually announced:

'It's got what it takes.'

Janos put another canvas on the easel, a sitting nude.

'Lovely,' said Hancock, 'lovely. You've got the real flesh tints there.'

Janos glanced at Mrs Hancock.

'It's very good, I'm sure. But I wouldn't like to have it.'

'*No one's asking you to, dear. And, anyway, you don't need to, you've got a long, long mirror.*' Hancock measured with his raw hands to show how long it was against his wife's body. She blushed, but did not altogether hide her smile.

We looked at a few more paintings. In front of each, Hancock either bantered with his wife or else asked questions and expressed admiration. When we sat down again he said:

'*Well, you are certainly a lucky man.*'

'*How is that?*'

'*Because you can work here all the time.*' Hancock looked round and up at the studio. '*I'm always telling Vee. The artist is the happiest man alive.*'

APRIL 6

The Waves has become nothing more than a pattern. The colours have lost all their appetite for meaning. None whatsoever. I am as familiar with that canvas as with the ink blue of the studio door. Would that I could bang it shut and forget it.

I think of Courbet's seascapes. It is wrong to believe that it was any easier for him. The only artists for whom it has been *comparatively* easy are those working in an inflexible religious tradition; for them to doubt their work was to doubt the power of their God – and so they didn't. It was not any easier for Courbet, but the problems were more tangible. For us everything, except the paint on the end of our brushes, is somewhat intangible. Our analyses, our tradition, our audience, our aims. If, from Cézanne onwards, we have created anything – then we have really created it.

APRIL 10

It is salutary to remember that the weather is only five miles thick. It is only the earth's casing – as temperament is ours.

APRIL 11

The wretchedly wayward heart. Why should a newly washed head of hair set it lungeing against the bars of its cage – when by all reason and logic only the old loyalties can lead to peace and calm? Why should a newly washed head of hair so preposterously seem like the pure landscape of an early summer morning, when the sky is skin blue – if flesh were ever naturally that colour – and one wakes like Adam with the heavy premonition of Eve filling the whole day? When we have solved the problems of work and sustenance, when we have leisure, maybe we shall still be faced with the problem of those premonitions: the problem even of how to forget a newly washed head of golden hair!

I suspect that this refers to Mrs Hancock.

APRIL 14

If you draw a series of parallel lines closely together, and then another series across them at an angle, you have the simplest visual example of the dialectical process. Cross-hatching as they call it. You have the first series of line, then you have the second series in opposition to the first. But out of the two you get a series of diamonds.

Now, if you look at these diamonds, remembering that every one has had to be drawn, you are overwhelmed by the length and complexity of the task. The diamonds are like the future we work for. Yet, courage. The first series of lines is there. All we have to do is to cross them.

APRIL 17

I have begun re-working *The Waves*. An object that sinks through water passes through architecture as definite as a chancel but as mobile as light. It is easy to contrast structure with movement: but to make structure *become* movement! The Cubists discovered the problem, but they only outlined the answer. They brought everything to the surface: now half of what they brought must be pushed back.

Brighton is one of the few places that Diana and I both enjoy: she the Regency architecture and the antique shops, and I all the traffic of ice-cream sellers and limousines in front of the sea. It was at Brighton, I think, that the idea of this painting first came to me. Underneath one of the piers, looking at the iron legs recording the distance above the water in one way and under it in another. But I didn't begin to visualize the painting then; that was not till after I had been to the aquarium. And the actual need to paint it didn't come till later still – when I was watching the gulls above the river at Greenwich. Then I saw exactly what I am now still looking for.

MAY 3

The canvas is finished. It is several weeks since I wrote in this book. And now re-reading what I wrote about this six square metres of rough canvas, I cannot help smiling. It is like hearing a recording of my conversations with a woman – about art, places, politics – when all I really wanted to say was 'You are lovely – come home with me.'

Now at last she is here – the canvas. And fortunately because it is a canvas and not a woman, I now have no regret, no guilt in taking another and beginning again – talking about art, places, politics.

Yet, in fact, that is not quite true. Between works you do suffer guilt. You come back to the increased rent and the telephone bill. You come back to what the petit-bourgeois calls reality. The artist is imagined to be a kind of Titan, strong, independent, free – even if propertyless. In fact, he is a dependant. Patronage has been reduced to a kind of charity – which is insufficient to go round. For the rest there is the economic vocation of teaching! For those who do not qualify for the small charity or for the small sinecure, there are their women: the wives or mistresses who earn to keep their men at the easel. Or there are the occasional friends with a little money who, if they have some to spare, buy a picture or commission a portrait, because a straight gift would be an insult. He is like a jail-bird, the artist, whom the few people that help him believe was innocent or unjustly sentenced.

It is believed that the artist has a sense of triumph when he has created a work that he knows to be good. In fact, what he sometimes has is a sense of vindication; sometimes he thinks, 'I am justifying my support.' Most of the while, however, he is guilty, longing for an eternity of time in which to work and in which guilt will not rush him as it does now. The artist who does not feel these things is a parasite.

The artist exists by virtue of the sacrifices of others. No wonder we grasp at Stalin saying he is 'the engineer of the soul.'

Engineers exist by virtue of the needs of others. Perhaps there is too much steel in Stalin's definition. But dependence is work.

As for the successful – Picasso, Léger, Brancusi. Look at their lives, not their present prices. They have all been scarred by the early humiliation of dependence. And today they all know that what they have, has been won in a lottery, not paid for in recognition of what has been earned.

Shortly after Janos had finished The Waves, *I suggested to him that he should enter it for the Sports Association Competition which I had then just heard about. There was £8,000 in prizes. He agreed, and Diana asked who the judges were going to be. I told her it had not been settled. But my suggestion made us light-hearted that night. We all explained what we would do with a couple of thousand, and drank wine and planned a trip to Italy. Later the Hancocks came in and were certain that Janos would win the prize. Diana said she would write to a cousin in Rome about accommodation. We often made such plans without really believing in them.*

MAY 10

What a difference the sun being out makes. The women, gossiping on the pavements, rock their prams up and down, and their babies' eyes are screwed up tight against the dazzle. The lovers looking in the jeweller's window, find it too hot to hold hands. Somewhere a girl on a swing is carried from the shade into the sunlight, from the sunlight into the shade.

MAY 12

Max came to borrow some money. I didn't. Then he went on about how we had changed since the old days in Berlin and about how now we have letter-boxes instead of open doors, and bank accounts and suits – and no spirit. You have made yourself believe you are a success, he said, and I am delighted to be a failure. But twenty years ago we wouldn't have thought in terms of either of those words. And he shook his head and smiled his tap-dancer's smile.

Max is incorrigible and I love him for that. As when he is reminded that it is Good Friday, and he stops and looks down at

49

his polished, dandy shoes and says, 'Poor chap! Poor chap!' But he is also tragic, and for that I hate him.

There is a time when every refugee lives in a no-man's-land. He must. Yet his mind is not there. It is backwards in regret, forwards in fear or hope. But Max has camped there in a no-man's-land now for twenty years. The way he has made it cosy with his nonchalance, his charm and his hand-made shoes, strikes many, I suppose, as heroic. In fact, it is detestable. He has no sense of duty or responsibility towards anything except his past, which has now become nothing but his pride. A refugee is nothing until he ceases to be one. Max has tried to turn it into an honourable profession. Consequently he has become the most parochial man I know.

The only thing to be said in his favour is that I can tell him this. He has not adopted the English attitude to friendship which precludes love on the one hand and the right to attack fiercely on the other. Friends have a duty to attack – to tear the pretensions off like dressings from a wound that needs the light. The English understand none of this. If you are friends with a man in England, as we understand the word *friend*, you are considered a homosexual.

Max, who was once a comedian in Berlin, worked for the monitoring service of the B.B.C. Although he was at least ten years younger than Janos, they had known each other in Germany. Whenever I saw them together, usually at the studio, they quarrelled, but it was, as Janos suggests, quarrelling based on some kind of understanding. At this time Max was living with a girl called Barbara who was always leaving him. He would complain about her to Janos.

'You have a wife, a home, children. Strictly speaking, you haven't any children, I know. But you would have, if you wanted them. I have nothing. Not even a proper place to live in. You know Mary Levinson is having a baby? Well, she is. And so we had to leave. They gave us three month's warning. Though I must say I think they could have given us a little more. When you're six months gone, you more than know it. Indeed, I'd already seen what was happening myself and was looking forward to having a child in the house. I thought it might be a good influence on Barbara: bring

out her maternal instincts. But no. One morning Mary said she was
very sorry but they would need our room. I said I was very sorry,
too, for myself and very glad for her. Weeks went by and we were
still there – we just couldn't find another place. Every time Mary
passed me she stuck her tummy out at me in a kind of reproach. The
bigger she got the smaller she wanted me to feel. Eventually
Barbara heard from somebody at the office of a very large room
going. But where? In Balham. Do you know Balham? It's the kind
of place that a ghost of a tram – if you could get on it with all the
corpses – would take you to on an all-night ticket. Every morning
Barbara has to get right across London to Warren Street by nine.
That means getting up at seven. Imagine the smell of a fried egg in
your bedroom at 7 a.m. She eats it on the dressing-table while she
does her hair. I just bear it for her sake, by putting my head under
the pillow. Then I got transferred on to night duty. And Barbara
started visiting her mother – who lives suspiciously near at Ken-
nington. This mother, as you know, thinks I'm the Devil incarnate.
So night after night she gets at Barbara, telling her she's meant for
better things. The end was the other night. I came back, to that
crypt, just as it was morning. She'd gone. There was a note on the
table. "I've taken your advice – Barbara." So there we are –
another end to what was once a beginning.'

MAY 15

What I wrote the other night about Max made me go on
thinking about him.

I have always fought in myself against everything that he has
become: right from the beginning, because after that there is no
one place where you can begin to fight. Every time that I have
arrived in a new city or a new country, I have been tempted to
establish myself – in my own eyes at least – with the memory of
what little security, prestige, achievement I had won in the last
place. How many hundred canvases did I leave in Berlin? And
always I have resisted this. I have not denied my past, and now,
as I grow old, I remember more than I used to. But I have clung
to the idea of the present being a culmination. I have never
allowed myself a sense of either tragic or relieved anti-climax.
The temptation takes you in many ways.

You arrive somewhere, alone. And then you want to take out

your memories, which are also dreams, and hang them round your room – like pictures. And between each picture you think of placing an imaginary mirror with your own face in it. That is how you furnish a room with the past. And for a little while it would even be an inspiration. But I have preferred – even if I have had no money and only a few words of the new language – to walk the new streets. The staring eyes of those who have noticed me – an obvious foreigner – have challenged me, and I have always accepted that challenge. The friends and the enemies of the Communist or of the artist are the same in every country. But to begin with, one must prove oneself and them. The process of learning is the process of constantly beginning again.

Or it works in another way. You see what you believe in going wrong. You see stupid, cruel mistakes. And you think to yourself this is not what I meant, this is not how I dreamt about it. And this is another kind of temptation. If you are fighting for something new, you are fighting for a vision. But when this vision becomes reality you must be prepared for much of the newness to hurt and shock you. Somewhere Gorki said the same. You must be prepared for this as a mother must know that her son will hurt her and leave her and destroy her world before she can become truly proud of him. Men are rough, both sons and lovers. And even to have a son you must take a rough man. We cannot be Virgin Marys. Yet when the world is very rough it is easier to be a spinster and only dream and judge. How many spinster artists and spinster intellectuals there are today!

And even now the temptations remain, here after twenty years in London. You see a young girl trotting like a pony down the street. You follow her with your eyes. And despite your old man's hair, you remember how when you were a student and a hero of the revolution and a comrade in a foreign city you made love for love and hope; and you think: I am still the same, I still belong to the same world. Then, supposing later you meet this girl at a friend's party and she smiles at you and almost says out loud that she thinks you are a romantic fellow who has seen so much, it is very hard then to act older than you feel. But if you don't, you will use her as a pony for taking you back to your past.

Why not? Because afterwards you will be alone with only your old blood pumping and dreaming. I do not mean this in a Puritan or Calvinistic sense. It is no law of God this. It is only a rule for elderly romantics who are also *émigrés*. And today every artist is forced to be a romantic, even though he may struggle with all his might for classicism.

MAY 20

I went to have what is left of my hair cut on the way back from the School. It was a newsagent's barber's that I had never discovered before, near the bus-stop. The barber was an Italian, and we talked of the Queen and then of Garibaldi. I watched him in the mirror over the basin as he worked. Every so often he stepped back to squint at my hair, his head on one side, his eyes screwed up. The gesture was exactly the same as a painter's when he steps back to look at his canvas. He wanted to see what he had done freshly, he wanted to see it in the best possible and most flattering light, but he also wanted to see it truthfully. That's the conflict of aim that makes us squint. But it is a gesture not only confined to barbers and painters. It is the world-wide gesture of men measuring their original work.

MAY 23

Another speech of Laszlo's is reported in *Népszava*.

'The validity of Socialist Realism, at any given stage in its development, must be judged according to the degree in which it arouses the consciousness of the working class to an awareness of their heroic role in the historical transformation of their society. Art which fails to do this is either the work of conscious reactionary propagandists or of the bourgeois formalists. Some claim that the formalist is only guilty of a fault of omission. Unfortunately such opinions reveal a total blindness to the objective, political reality of our time. It is well known that today when Socialism has been established in the U.S.S.R., China and the Peoples' Democracies, a sense of social hopelessness can only occur on the basis of rejecting the achievements of Socialism. Thus, the pessimism and escapism of the Formalists places them, whether they wish it or not, in the camp of reaction.'

53

What would he think of my *Waves* – moving past like clouds over mountains?

At heart I have remained as we were when we were students. But Laszlo has shouldered heavy responsibilities. One can feel them in his conventional words. Centralized, organizational words. They lumber across the page, clearing irrelevancies out of the way like bulldozers. And in that is the difficulty for the artist. The artist's justification lies in creating new relevancies; but it takes a long time. To create a heavy industry in five or ten years is an heroic but possible aim. To create a heavyweight art in the same time is impossible. Laszlo must know this. What he is really doing, and probably he realizes it, is defending the new steel plants, the new uranium mines. If I could, I would defend them with him.

I remember him at our favourite museum café. He was late for every rendezvous. He would leap off the tram as it passed the café, bang through the glass doors and join us in our corner, full of earnest apologies. 'Marta,' he would shout to the girl behind the counter, 'one goulash and two plates. Jansci'll share mine with me.' And I would eat and he would talk and forget to eat. 'I'll tell you what we're doing, our generation – painters, like Jansci, and sculptors, writers and poets. We're all the guardians of a small girl. And our job is to feed her, bring her up, teach her, so that one day she becomes a marvellous woman, like Marta here, but with everything Marta hasn't got or doesn't know as well. And then the people will fall in love with her. Perhaps we'll never see the wedding. But it'll take place. The marriage of art and the people!' People do not talk like that any longer. But then we were not only young, we were living in a young time. Today I do not have the impression that the time, anyway in Europe, is so young.

MAY 27

Candy pink and ochre, just touched with cobalt to turn it rancid, give off more heat, more temperature, than pure cadmium or chrome. Heat is a question of the relationship of the blues to the rest. Heat is resonance not brilliance. Compare copper with gold. Poussin used blues to make his classic flesh eternally warm, eternally young. What his mantles did to his figures, I want the water to do to my swimmer.

Janos often painted pictures in a series. After he had finished The Waves, *he began on a canvas of a swimmer which contained many of the innovations he had made in the earlier picture.*

JUNE 22

For several weeks I have been working on *The Swimmer*, and have written nothing. It is a large canvas, 2 by 3 metres. That is the equivalent of tilling 10 hectáres.

JUNE 24

Left the canvas today, to renew my ideas by drawing. Susan came to pose. She is a sweet girl, over-brimming with keenness. She slings her body into a pose, holds it, and then, if I let her, bombards me with questions of what I think of Léger or Le Corbusier. 'Is a modern Classicism possible?' she'll ask as I trace the parabola of her buttock through her intervening thigh to connect with that of her stomach. Then when we rest, she sits with her chin on her knees, and her breasts squashed together, telling me how hopelessly the rest of the teachers teach at the school. I doubt, however, whether she'll ever become a painter. She'll marry one instead. Perhaps the one thing the art schools do well here is to train painters' wives. It is a vocation.

Dear Diana. She is loyal, but I can see in her extra upright walk how she unconsciously disapproves. Not through Puritanism. Not even through jealousy. It is the casual informality she disapproves of. She believes artists should only draw nudes of their wives – or their mistresses. Anything else means a loss of dignity all round. She always brings out the silver tea-pot and the best family tea-cups. 'Milk or lemon?' she asks, then hands a cup delicately to Susan, and begins to talk about anything outside the studio. She never looks at the drawings or refers to the afternoon's work in any way.

Nevertheless, one of Janos's best nudes is of Diana (she looks about seventeen) painted just after they were married.

It is the most profound activity of all, this one of drawing. And the most demanding. It is when I draw that I regret the weeks, the years perhaps, that I have wasted. If, as in the fairy stories, I could grant a gift to a child who was to become a painter, it would be a long life, so that he might master this activity of drawing. What so few people realize is that the painter, unlike the writer or the architect or the designer, is both creator and executant of his art. He needs two lives. And, above all, to master drawing. Nearly every artist can draw when he has made a discovery. But to draw in order to discover – that is the god-like process, that is to find effect and cause. The power of colour is nothing compared to the power of the line; the line that does not exist in nature but which can expose and demonstrate the tangible more sharply than can sight itself when confronted with the actual object. To draw is to know by hand – to have the proof that Thomas demanded. Out of the artist's mind through the point of a pencil or pen comes proof that the world is solid, material. But the proof is never familiar. Every great drawing – even if it is of a hand or the back of a torso, forms perceived thousands of times before – is like the map of a newly discovered island. Only it is far easier to read a drawing than a map; in front of a drawing it is the five senses that make a surveyor.

All great drawing is drawing by memory. That is why it takes so long to learn. If drawing were transcription, a kind of script writing, it could be taught in a few years. Even before a model, you draw from memory. The model is a reminder. Not of a stereotype that you know by heart. Not even of anything you can consciously remember. The model is a reminder of experiences you can only formulate and therefore only remember by drawing. And those experiences add up to the sum total of your awareness of the tangible, three-dimensional, structural world. A blank page of a sketch-book is a blank, white page. Make one mark on it, and the edges of the pages are no longer simply where the paper was cut, they have become the borders of a microcosm. Make two marks on it of uneven pressure and the whiteness ceases to be whiteness and becomes opaque three-dimensional space that must be made less opaque and more and

56

more lucid by every succeeding mark. That microcosm is filled
with the potentiality of every proportion you have ever perceived or sensed. That space is filled with the potentiality of
every form, sliding plane, hollow, point of contact, passage of
separation you have ever set eye or hand on. And it does not
stop even there. For, after a few more marks, there is air, there is
pressure and therefore there is bulk and weight. And this scale
is then filled with the potentiality of every degree of hardness,
yieldingness, force of movement, activeness and passiveness that
you have ever buried your head in or knocked it against. And
from all this you must select in a few minutes, as nature did
through millennia, in order to create a human ankle, a human
arm-pit with the pectoral muscle burying itself like an underground stream, or the bough of a tree. From all this you must
select the one lock and one key. I think I would grant three
lives not two.

JULY 4

We all went to a swimming-pool near Epsom – Diana, John,
the Hancocks and myself. It was Hancock's happy idea, and we
went in his van. Since you are painting *The Swimmer*, he said,
you should see the real thing. His wife is a superb performer and
comes out of the water like Botticelli's Venus. But it was also
the whole carefree afternoon I enjoyed so much. Thousands of
people were streaming out of London, dressed in brightly
coloured cottons and silks – charabancs, motor-bikes, bicycles,
tandems, cars, lorries full of children. Everywhere you looked
people were lying on the green grass; some in each other's
arms: some with newspapers over their faces. It was like seeing
a straight play that the sun had suddenly turned into a comedy.
For a few hours the silver mascots on the bonnets of the sports
cars were a hundred times more meaningful than all the Greek
and Etruscan fragments in the British Museum – even if they
had been put together and made complete again. The conviction
that art must always be modern was justified. The sun made
everything modern.

At the pool the girls shrieked raucously, and the speed of their
diving bodies made their small costumes look like the brilliant
plumage of parrots. My canvas was right.

Certainly everybody was happy that afternoon, although, in retrospect, it is hard to explain why. The day before I had heard that I was to serve on the jury of the Sports Association Competition and that one of the other judges was to be Sir Gerald Banks. This greatly amused Janos and put Diana into a state of confused excitement; on the one hand she was delighted that I should have a chance of championing Janos's work, on the other hand she was appalled all over again that Janos had so queered his pitch with Banks. I explained to her that this would make no difference, because Banks wouldn't know who had painted The Waves, *but she remained unconvinced. Possibly it was simply the weather that intoxicated us. It was, as Janos describes, a perfect July Saturday. The swimming-pool was crowded with frivolous couples. Janos sat on the balcony, leaning forward to watch us. Len Hancock, who looked preposterous with his short trunks round the middle of his exaggeratedly knobbly six-foot-six body, tried to carry Diana on his shoulders. At first she protested violently. But after they had swum, she lost her embarrassment. Mrs Hancock, waving to us from the highest diving-board each time before she somersaulted off, dived time and time again, like a bird out of her cage. After about an hour, we went up to the balcony to greet Janos.*

'Have you ever fallen in love in the sea, Mr Lavin? You can fall no farther. It's an A1 experience, believe me. That's how I met Vee.' Hancock put his hand on his wife's shoulder.

'Oh, Len, don't be so silly. Don't believe a word, Mr Lavin. He just says these things.'

'I am sure every man would fall in love with you in the water, Mrs Hancock.'

'Too true,' said Len.

'Why don't you come in, too?' asked Diana.

'Oh yes, do. It's ever so warm.'

'Come on. Practise what you paint!'

'I'll go and get you a costume,' said Diana, 'it'll do you a world of good.'

'Too true,' added Len.

And so he was persuaded. The hired bathing costume barely fitted him, but his body was surprisingly athletic, with only a very slight stomach. He walked along the side of the bath towards us,

58

rubbing his black-haired arms and grinning. His two bushes of grey hair above each ear looked like an after-thought.

'If I sink, I expect the rescue.'

'Vee's got a gold medal for life-saving and I can walk there,' said Hancock, putting his hand up to his chin to show where the water would come to.

Janos dived in and came up with his wild hair flattened.

'It is not so cold.'

'Water cooled,' shouted Len.

'You can dive,' said Mrs Hancock. 'Come and try a higher one.'

Janos clambered out, puffing a little.

'Just one time.'

He climbed up to the highest board, looking very serious, as if he were entering for a competition. Diana waved to him a little anxiously. He put his arms above his head and then – quite unexpectedly – just jumped, coming down feet first and holding his nose.

'Ah, the artist!' Hancock exclaimed in admiration.

JULY 7

Laszlo has been executed.

I can neither work nor write. I walk and go round and round the circles of my mind. There is no one I can refer to.

There is a Sicilian song. A song of imprisonment.

> *It is time to let us go, it is dark,*
> *The skin of the cat begins to shine.*

There was never going to be a chance of my seeing you again.

AUGUST 5

Two a.m. in the morning. Everything in the studio absolutely still. Everything is clearly going to survive the night. If I listen very sharply, I can hear Diana's breathing. She has a hell of a life. How much I would like to see her hopeful again. Perhaps we should have had children. Then she would have had the allies she needs to fight me. It would have been a more equal fight. I have cowed her with failure, as other men might have done with force. And the fact that for me it is not failure is for

59

her all the more embittering. She suffers both the failure and my reproach to her for considering it so. And I suffer her resignation. Thus, we can quarrel about whether to put a 60-watt or 100-watt electric-light bulb into a lamp. The Budapest prison had no electricity.

I do not write with complete frankness even here. I am conscious of that. But it does not trouble me. Confessing is a supine activity. The death hour precludes any further action. Was that your conclusion, Laci? But until then it would be better to act frankly, and one acts more frankly by avoiding the excavation of all one's motives. Frank action is the result of frankly facing the result. The frankest actions of my life have all been political. I must still believe that. Did you believe that even when you confessed?

I can see two stars through the skylight. Once this would have seemed the very summer of the night and the dawn a year's ending. Proserpine returning only to the underworld of her sleep, from which she could be brought back by a single kiss. Now, I would like to believe that it is only an interval between two working days. I have always hated leisure. The imminence of the future we believed in made it impossible for a moment to be wasted. We wasted many, of course. But we never realized it. There are nights and there are working days. Even now when the English say 'week-end', I have to make myself remember that they mean two days' retirement. But supposing a whole life were wasted?

AUGUST 11

The Waves has been taken away for the Competition. I looked at it before it went. It is impossible for me to imagine how it will strike other people. Diana simply asked, 'Is it finished now?' Max made a joke of it, 'Where's Britannia?' he laughed. Len Hancock said, 'It's very nice, very nice indeed; you must have worked hard on that one.' John, as usual, admired because he needs to believe in my genius to prove some obscure point that dominates his mind. I worked on it whilst Laszlo was being interrogated. Perhaps the circling gulls in my painting even came from a memory of the circling pigeons in his poem. But my sea is impersonal. And his crowd was human. He has been harried, accused, executed. And I, am I drowning in my art? Must circumstances make all of us Romantics? I am haunted by your last hours, Laci. Did you think then like you wrote, as a defender of the steel plants which you were accused of sabotaging: or like the youth jumping off the tram, the noise of which you now knew you could never hear again – like the youth, charging into the museum café? But there was another café, in Vienna, where Paul was shot in the back room – Paul who had informed on five of us who were arrested before they could reach Vienna. Laci, were you?

AUGUST 14

I should never have been a painter. Only the moral obligation to work makes me persist.

AUGUST 15

When ideas and actions are judged by their intention or sincerity instead of by their results, it is one of the paradoxes of human nature that confidence tricksters thrive. Laci, were you?

Anything is justified in art, but everything must be related. There is nothing that the painter need be forbidden to do. Nothing at all. But when he has finished, what he has done must be judged in relation to the always different and always present struggle of men to realize their potentiality more fully. Did you understand that, Laci? It is not simple.

The Jury for the Sports Association Competition consisted of Sir Gerald Banks; Guy Hunter, the critic and expert on Beardsley, Swinburne and the art of the nineties; Cuthbert Lyons, well-known apologist for abstract art and author of The Machine as Symbol; *a Mr Wilmot, who was the representative of the Sports Association; and myself. There were 6,000 entries from which we had to select 100 for exhibiting and four prize-winners. We sat in a row of chairs and porters carried the paintings past us whilst we watched. As each painting moved past we voted for it to be labelled Rejected, Accepted or Doubtful. Sir Gerald Banks sat well back in his chair with his arms folded, and confined himself to saying 'In' on the few occasions when he thought a work was interesting. Guy Hunter,*

61

young, with a round face and a silver-topped stick, leaning against the back of his chair, supported a work by saying 'Yes, yes,' Cuthbert Lyons, in drain-pipe trousers and with a crew cut, leaned forward with his elbows on his knees and his thin white face scowling in concentration. 'Pro,' he said, when he was in favour of a picture. Mr Wilmot said nothing.

Janos's painting, larger than most of the others, moved past us, carried by two porters. 'Yes,' I said. 'Ac-ac-academic,' said Lyons, but since nobody else said anything it was Accepted. Our average was about three paintings a minute, and so after three days (each member of the Jury was paid £80 for the job), we were down to the final task of selecting the prize-winners from amongst the Accepteds and the Doubtfuls. By this time our judgement was somewhat blunted. Hunter, giggling, said, 'I feel just like a priest, don't you know, after a fiesta. Only a confession of sodomy can startle me now.' Mr Wilmot plied us with whiskies, and we each made our own list of the four prize-winners. A few selections overlapped, so we were faced with sixteen canvases from which to choose four. I think that at this stage I was the only one to vote for The Waves. Each of us then defended our choices and sought to persuade the others. Sir Gerald appealed to our collective sense of responsibility, 'We are not here to encourage possible promise but, surely, to adjudicate on achievement.' Lyons demonstrated his points physically by moving his arms over each canvas to show how 'the membranes of space' became 'architectonic'. Hunter, seeking for an image, found 'intoxicating as a perfume by Guerlain'. At the end of two hours six paintings were left, and The Waves was one of them. We paused to go and get something to eat. 'Tell me,' Banks asked, 'that painting of the sea you think so much of, do you know who painted it? It's a mature work, obviously, but I can't put a name to it.' For a moment I hesitated, then decided that it would help rather than hinder. 'Janos Lavin,' I said. 'So that's it,' and he stared into the distance for a moment. We returned to the job. 'I'm going to vote against that sea thing,' said Hunter. 'It's too cold, don't you know, mechanical.' 'And me,' Lyons agreed. 'Far too much of a compromise. An abstraction tarted up to be figurative.' Banks looked above their heads. 'I like it,' he announced firmly. 'It has character. It's independent.' Thus the decisive vote was Mr Wilmot's. We all looked at him and he screwed up his eyes at the canvas, 'Well, as I see it, gentlemen, we'd like to see the prizes go to the really advanced chaps, you know the really modern. I'd say this was a bit quiet.'

AUGUST 25

I am restless and I sleep too late. Diana watches me, astounded at what she imagines to be my reaction to the competition result.

Through a slit in a garden fence the sunlight falls on a patch of bare, dug earth, the colour of sacking, and the thin golden line of the sunlight on the earth is like a stitched row of golden seedlings. White walls are rarer in London than wild flowers.

AUGUST 30

Went to the National Gallery and looked at the Bellini *Agony* and the Titian *Bacchus and Ariadne*. They were not gods. It is only the scholars who think them that. Even the worst and humblest painter need feel no awe in front of his great predecessors. We can only learn from the success of our equals. It is the eternal, damned comparative measuring of talent or genius that vitiates art by breeding doubt and by separating ability from its usage. Titian would have acknowledged me, or, if he hadn't, it would have been because he didn't like my face, or because I cheated him out of a job or girl. In front of a Titian, if it is a good one, I become prouder. I am reminded of what it is to be a painter. And if I am also reminded of the relative failure of my own paintings, this is unimportant; the sense of fraternity is stronger. Only other painters can understand this. Those who think that art is transportable, timeless, universal, understand it least of all. They put a Hindu sculpture next to a Michelangelo, and marvel at the fact that in both cases the woman has two breasts! But it is the differences which are essential to our sense of fraternity. Each of us works for different ends, under different pressures; a few of them personal, most of them social and historical. Without these differences we could never accept the difference in achievements. The only thing we share is the magnitude of the difficulty we face: the technical difficulty. The historians would even deny that, of course. They would contrast a craftsman in the Byzantine tradition which barely changed for centuries with the revolutionaries of the Renaissance. But I do not accept this as the whole truth. We all face the same problem of coordinating our eyes and our hands with our minds. We are all athletes whose limbs are images. And the athletes of every age have something in common. A Byzantine mosaicist pauses to reflect on the last ordained tessera he has inserted; a Renaissance painter pauses to reflect on whether his proportions, his counterpoint, can be made more unified; a Baroque artist pauses to examine whether he can tense even further; Delacroix pauses to reflect on the romantic alchemy of his colour; Cézanne pauses to reflect again on whether he is still being faithful to his little elusive sensation; we today pause to reflect on whether our severity might be made more severe; and in every one of these pauses the artist faces the same difficulty – it is the difficulty that unites us – the difficulty of making the intangible tangible, of creating a cold form to contain our fervent content. All of us know that difficulty so profoundly that we would all recognize its nature despite the totally different considerations that fill our pauses. Down the road there is an old man who sits in a chair under the porch of his front door to enjoy the sun. He is very old. In fact, he is dying. And because I know this, every time I pass him I pass the time of day with him. I tell him he is getting brown in the sun. Or he asks me about the price of the vegetables in my shopping bag – once he lived in the country – and I answer him at length and with great warmth. Why do I do this? It is a natural reaction. Soon he will die, he will be dead as Laszlo, and I want him between now and then, and perhaps even at the moment of dying, to have good thoughts, not of me personally, but of the living, of the world he leaves. I want to give him reason for thinking the best possible thoughts. And so it has been for every artist. The old man, sunning through his last days, is not, strictly speaking, a necessary reminder for us artists. We know it without having to pass him on the way back from the greengrocer's. We have all wanted others to take away the best possible thoughts that we can struggle to make manifest. And in that is our fraternity. To all those who have not faced the difficulty of it, our common aim will sound so vague that it becomes unreal. But was it so unreal, Laci? Or were you? Let me think again of the Titian and Bellini.

64

For the Renaissance artist draperies were what paint and drawing themselves have become for us. Their folds have become our brushmarks or, for those of us who are suspicious of gesture, our manner of analysing planes. Renaissance drapery was as arbitrary as the facets of the Cubists. The robe that Christ wears in the Bellini is simultaneously a manner of analysing the structure of his body, of unifying him with the merciless landscape where the same fissures are made of rock instead of cloth, and of expressing the moment of reckoning when time locks like the slowest glacier, yet moves more terribly than the fastest shooting star. After you were sentenced, Laci, you waited for such time to kill you.

Let me think again of the Titian. It is the same. Drapery has nothing to do with dress in that painting either. It entwines, flows over, trails beyond and glorifies the bodies just as three hundred years later Renoir made the light do. Or even as fifty years later Titian himself did in that *Shepherd and Nymph* in Vienna. Ah, the milk of the light in that canvas I haven't seen for twenty-five years! And the woman's hand plucking at her own arm like the hand of her lover! How the old man dreamt! After the sleeping draught and the last visit of the brisk, cheerful night nurse in the old people's ward, how many octogenarians mutter beside that shepherd and, putting their old hand into the glove of that young one, play whilst the shepherd pipes the hit-tune of their heyday and the broken tree behind bears witness to their age and to the temperature chart above their bed? We have all been simple. What is complex beyond measure is our technique. Titian said a great painter needed only three colours. But I count vision as technique, too. Titian as a randy old man is no different from my friend down the road watching the girls walk through his last summer. Genius is never a case apart. It is utterly opposed to mania. The genius bears the full weight of what is common, of what exists hundreds and thousands of times over. But he watches himself. That is the largest part of his technique, and it is what separates him from others. We all forget continually. The genius, because he watches himself, remembers. He naïvely remembers his dreams, he ruthlessly remembers his real experiences, and gradually, very gradually, he learns to remember the exact nature of his mistakes and successes as a man applying paint to a flat surface. And so he recognizes what others have felt but never known. Technique and genius are nothing more nor less than recognition.

I have tried to sleep, but I cannot. When I close my eyes, I see the Titian canvas in Vienna. But behind the figures in the scrubbed, unfinished milky dawn light of the sky, I see too much of Vienna. I hear the buckets of a near-by concierge early in the morning after we had killed Paul who had betrayed us.

Let me think again of the woman in the foreground. Two buttocks like pearls. There are two kinds of remembering. There is the Giorgione Venus in Dresden. And there is the Titian. Giorgione remembers the figure of a woman who is already departed, already absent, already subject to the idealization of memory that begins as soon as one begins to remember one's memories. I love that Giorgione. But she hangs there like a crescent moon remembered on a cloudy night. She is a reconstruction. And so she fits into an ordained shape. She is anticipation and memory, but she is not fact. Her awkward limbs slide into a total form of perfect symmetry. She is reconstructed, albeit perfectly – there's the point: not imperfectly – from the imprint she left on the grass. But not so the Titian with two buttocks like two pearls. There are elisions there, too, but they are tribute only to the unreasonable adoration one feels in face of the fact; they are a tribute to the unknown quality that jostles the known facts – not to the kind of memory that does not jostle at all. The Giorgione is a virgin dream, poignant in its ignorance. The Titian is the memory of a woman who was briefly once all that the picture pretends. The point is too fine perhaps for any except an *emigré* who both dreams of and remembers the women of his own country. Katinka. My age.

SEPTEMBER 15
Worked all the morning on *The Swimmer*. The School in the afternoon. I posed the model on a bicycle. The students reacted well, after their first titter of laughter.

SEPTEMBER 16
It is very late and I have just played a trick on myself. I have worked on the plate of a new etching – a man carrying a ladder.

I have made the first print. But I will not look at it till the morning. This will be a reason for getting up early.

SEPTEMBER 18

Hardwick has heard about my posing the model on a bicycle and made a joke about it in the staff-room. Clearly he disapproved. 'You'd get very few models to do it,' he added, 'and certainly none of the experienced ones.' He ought to have a job in the Ministry of Trade.

A new teacher has arrived at the School. He takes still-life painting and is an elderly man like myself. Yesterday I was reminded how old I was. Leaning backwards to try to see a part of the canvas as a whole, I fell off the steps. Nothing serious, just a bruise on my hips. But as I lay on the floor cursing, I could feel my heart banging like a bad engine.

This man is called Leonard Gough. He wears spectacles, and has a face like Rembrandt's father, everything worn away except what's in the skull-cap. The unusual thing about him is that he is stone deaf. One has to communicate with him by writing on a slip of paper. At lunch he sat next to me and passed me a note. DO YOU TEACH BECAUSE YOU WANT TO? I nodded and he continued to eat. Every so often he looked at me as if reckoning my reply against what he could see in my face. Then he passed me the slip of paper again. WHAT IS YOUR OWN WORK LIKE? Laughing, I wrote underneath – GOOD. When he had read it, he grasped my arm and smiled in a way that made me feel much younger than him. They say he is a brilliant teacher, and I can believe it, because instead of talking he must demonstrate. If all art schools were staffed by the dumb, the silent art might prosper.

The Minister of Culture has just made a speech about Laszlo. 'Under cover of his art, he worked for the enemies of Socialism.'

Hardwick was the Principal of the Art School at which Janos taught.

SEPTEMBER 23

Went over to Putney to see George's new works. What an

advantage his working-class origin gives him! He is preserved from all the charm of the dilettanti, who now take up art solely because they have what in the eighteenth century they would have been content to call Taste. His new paintings are good. He has obstinacy, which is the most necessary of all virtues under our siege conditions. The artist who comes from the working class or from any historically under-privileged group, nearly always arrives with this obstinacy or with a profound suspicion. But the last is fatal. It is suspicion and not any lack of sophisticated culture which damages such artists when they are damaged. I still remember Heinz in Berlin: the son of a railway worker and extraordinarily talented. But he was always afraid that there was some secret knowledge which all his contemporaries had been given along with their other privileges and which he had been deprived of. This led him to pointless, sterile efforts. He would paint a picture all in warm colours, and then again the same picture in exactly the same way but all in cool colours – just because he had read in some fool book that this was the secret of understanding colour. And if you criticized one of his paintings, he would frown and earnestly say, 'Yes, I know. I haven't learnt that yet.' As if every failure was the result of his lack of official education. Not so George. And June is an ideal painter's wife. Painters should marry cooks not sponsors.

George Trent, the thirty-two-year-old son of a Yorkshire miner, was the nearest Janos had to a pupil. They did not meet often, but George set great store by Janos's opinion. He probably made a little more money out of his painting than Janos because he was known amongst a few collectors and dealers as one of the New Young Realists. A label is half the battle.

On one occasion I went with Janos to see George's work – it was through me, as far as I can remember, that they first met.

George led us into the front room which was stripped of all furniture, and very cold despite the oil-stove, for it was winter. On the floor newspapers were laid out and leaning against the walls all the way round were unframed canvases.

As he opened the door, George stood aside with the air of a man who has conducted the main speakers on to the platform and for whom there is now nothing more to do except keep out of the way.

About twenty painted heads, mostly of Yorkshire working people, faced us.

Janos walked slowly round the room, and then squatted on his heels to study two or three pictures closely. One could see the bald patch on the top of his head, but from the back his hair was so thick that his ears were invisible. His long wrist shot out of his rucked-up sleeve, and he smudged his hand over a bit of the canvas.

'Good, good,' he muttered.

'It isn't what I'm after yet,' replied George, still by the door. 'But there's nothing to be done except to go on. You can't put your finger on it. Sometimes it comes right, sometimes not.'

Janos turned round towards him, still squatting on his heels, and laughed.

'A good painting, it comes like a thief in the night. No?'

Then after a while he began to talk about the paintings in detail:

'This head is very good, very good. I feel it is permanent.'

'I had a hell of a job with that. Painted it about six times.'

'Yes, yes, of course. I only feel it is permanent because it is all one. Always the pose and the expression must seem to be able to last as long as the paint and canvas themselves. If not, it is only a snapshot, a bit of stolen life. But this is not like that. The thick paint, the form, his complexion, the light, all the life this man has lived – they come together. They do not twist each other's arms. . . . But this, this, I do not like so much. The woman and the girl is good. But the staircase behind, it does not go back like they come forward. It is paint pattern, no more. Look. Here you feel the inches round the girl's ankle. It is only two brushmarks of thick paint, yet they have made the measure round that ankle. But you do not feel how many feet away the wall is behind them. It floats about – the wall; it does not find its place. And the hand here, it is a cut-off hand. Each finger is all right by each finger, but in the real hand you can feel the coming from the shoulder. Here you do not feel the coming from the shoulder. You have too much copied. You have not followed through to make again – to construct the arm. . . .'

Whilst he talked, Janos's hands moved over each picture, as though he was pulling threads out of it, or making giant stitches through its illusionary three-dimensional space. George stood beside him, listening and nodding his head. Slowly we moved round

*the room, examining painting after painting. Occasionally George
would speak, slowly, deliberately, but with his usual distrust of words.*

*' I see what you're getting at. I was thinking the other day. How
a blind man doesn't lack a sense of reality, you know? And that's
the kind of reality, if you see what I mean, that I want to get into
the paintings.'*

*After about three-quarters of an hour, the light began to fail and
we could see no more. We went back into the kitchen, Janos rubbing
his cold hands together. George's wife had come back from work and
was making tea.*

'Hello, Janos. What do you think of the new work?' she asked.

*'You know what I think of your husband. He has much to say –'
Janos began.*

*'That's what I'm always telling him,' she interrupted, her eyes
very wide open but her voice sharp. ' The trouble with George is that
he worries too much. Do you know, sometimes he even gets up in the
middle of the night, and goes down to potter about in the front
room there.'*

*George gave her a look to tell her to shut up. She looked back at
him with her wide eyes and laid down the bread-knife.*

*' Oh, I know I always say the wrong thing, but he' – and her
small hand pointed at her husband in mock accusation – 'he bottles
it all up like jerkuns.'*

'What about that cup of tea?' was George's reply.

*' You'll get it in a minute.' She threw him a smile like a paper
dart.*

*' But what do you really think?' she asked Janos again. Janos
was sitting by the kitchen table, crouched forward, warming his
hands in front of the electric fire on the floor. He looked up at June
and smiled at her reassuringly. There are a few people whose eyes,
unlike their lids, their brows, their cheek-bones, remain unmarked by
experience. Janos was one. His eyes smiled at June now as they must
at one time have smiled at his mother to reassure her that he had not
stolen the salami he'd brought back from school.*

' I think his pictures advance and get better,' he said.

SEPTEMBER 25

Worked all day on *The Swimmer*.

Tonight there was a sunset like a straightened rainbow, but

the arena in which this feat of strength had been accomplished was cloudless, deserted.

OCTOBER 8

I can talk about Laszlo to nobody. To the English a political execution is first and foremost a *primitive* act. Certainly they carry out political executions themselves, but only on primitive people – the Irish, the Africans, the Malays, people who have been misled into provoking them with unnecessary barbaric violence. They understand far more about murder. But to kill for a political principle – that is primitive and inconceivable. Civil war usually begins after national defeat. The English have forgotten what it is to experience either. From this comes their assumption that a person's nationality is the primary fact about him – coming even before sex, let alone class or political beliefs. I never fully realized that I was a Hungarian until I came to England.

During the last few days I have quarrelled with Diana on every possible occasion. The whole place is heavy with disappointment – like gas from a leaking pipe.

OCTOBER 14

The Swimmer is finished. It is good in parts. But the attempt to keep all the colours as equal as possible in tone makes a glance at it more rewarding than a concentrated study of it. And this maybe gives it an air of nostalgia that is so foreign to my purpose. It is very difficult to prevent dazzle becoming nostalgic.

Fra Angelico and Monet succeeded.

Several months after this, Janos re-worked on The Swimmer *canvas, heightening the tonal contrasts, and thus, in my opinion as well, improving the picture.*

OCTOBER 20

The Hancocks came round unexpectedly and John also brought some friends. Then a couple of students of mine, whom I've invited round once or twice, dropped in because they were passing. There were enough people for several conversations to continue at the same time. For once the studio was filled with voices. Diana was more animated than I have seen her for weeks. We all drank quite a lot of wine, and one of J's friends started singing Irish songs – which all sound like laments to me. But I could not share in it. I wanted to leave them all enjoying themselves and walk by myself. And then the thought of them happy in my studio would have been a good thought, even a comfort.

This entry is a surprise. Janos appeared light-hearted and convivial. Indeed, afterwards I congratulated myself on having the idea of taking my friends round to the studio – so cheering was the effect it seemed to have had on Janos. As for the singing, he sang some Hungarian songs himself, and also told several stories with considerable spirit. One, I remember, was about an old London woman whom he had seen in a pub, and who was watching a man teasing his dog with a ball. Suddenly the woman screamed across the bar at this man, 'When I see a man like that being cruel to animals, I pray God will find strength to strike him dumb, dead and paralysed!' 'The fortune of you English!' Janos added a little enigmatically.

As he left, Hancock drew me to one side and whispered that he wanted to talk business with me and would phone me. Can he really want to buy a painting?

NOVEMBER 4

I have begun planning and drawing for a new canvas. Four bathers out of the water at a Lido. During the Renaissance everyone accepted the symbol of goddesses. The modern nude is something quite different and began with Goya. Our goddesses can only be created from the pleasure of the people, for the whole beauty of goddesses is that they are anonymous.

NOVEMBER 12

Hardwick sent for me. 'I'm a little worried about some of your students,' he said, 'they're getting a bit too academic. Encourage them to go round the exhibitions rather more – not just the National Gallery all the time. I know you believe in a sound basis, but you can have too much of a good thing. They should keep up with the times. You understand?' I understood.

The only kind of modern dress which is really beautiful is that used for sport. Tennis skirts, cycling shorts, bikinis, ski-ing trousers, football shirts. You played on the wing, I as half-back. And after one match when we had scored three times in quick succession – you said we should both be footballers. You're a better half-back than you'll ever be a painter, you said. And a few years later: you're more than a friend. You're my truest comrade, you said.

And under the cover of your art, they say, you worked for the enemies of Socialism. You worked against your comrades. Many of us have always talked like that. But it was always nonsense. You can't work for anything under the cover of art. I can't even work for Socialism under the cover of my art. You can only work for something else under the cover of non-art. Art does not cover – it reveals. But I am edging away from the pain. You were a man as well as an artist. And a man can work for anything under every kind of cover. Also recently you were more an administrator than an artist, and an administrator can make mistakes which serve his enemies. I have always believed that those who exercise power must face the penalties of their mistakes. That does not happen under the class conspiracies of social democracy. A pension or a peerage are then the penalty of mistakes. The dictatorship of the proletariat must be a two-way process. The hard justice it serves must also extend to its leaders. In that lies our superior morality. But mistakes are not treason. An unsuccessful revolutionary does not become a reactionary because he is unsuccessful, even supposing his failure aids reaction. Our materialism cannot be reduced to Nothing Succeeds like Success. And if mistakes are punished by death, who learns?

You always struck your matches outwards. I remember that as I try to conjure you up and judge you. I try to see you the other side of this table on which my etching tools are lying. I would never have seen you again, anyway; or, at least, I never hoped that I would, though perhaps you would have come here to talk about Hungarian poetry to the P.E.N. Club. How guilty, Laci? Last night I dreamt there was only one more problem to solve. I forget what it was now. It is only facts I want, not testimonies of innocence or good intentions. How guilty, Laci?

Here what shocks everyone so much are the confessions. But I can remember enough not to be shocked by them, not even yours. Yet you must have believed there was no alternative, as desperate as any ever. For Romantics like you it is more difficult to lay down your reputation than your life. Possibly it's the same for all of us. You were desperate either because you knew you were totally innocent or because your confession was true. Your confession proves that you were either a traitor or a self-chosen martyr – not just a victim. Because if you were innocent and you had believed in the possibility of justice you would have protested. If you were innocent your confession means that you realized, perhaps that you always knew, that justice had been so compromised that to protest against yet another miscarriage of it would be to sow even more doubt, to endanger the Party. It has never been the rule for a confession to save the confessor's life. You, of course, knew that. So if you were innocent, why did you not die protesting? Your protest might have saved others and drawn attention to grave faults in the judiciary system. The only possible answer is that you were frightened of what you imagined might be the result of your protestation of innocence – or that you were tortured; but this I do not believe. You were frightened that your protest might encourage reaction, counter-revolution, disillusionment. But why should it? It could only do so if the whole judiciary system was so compromised that it could not afford to admit, even in one instance, what everybody correctly suspected or knew.

But supposing you were guilty. Supposing both suppositions are true. That there was grave injustice which drove you into opposition, so that against you there *was* justice in the charge. No. For then you would never have confessed. If you had already been driven into active opposition you would have had no qualms about the relatively minor danger of your protesting your innocence.

But in all this I assume that you were as I knew you. And, even more dangerously, I assume that I am now as you knew me thirty years ago. I speak as though we have both remained in the same position with the same standards. And had we spoken frankly to each other a few months ago over a trans-European telephone our words would not have belied this assumption. Few people change the name of their aims when once they have put a name to them. We would still have spoken about Socialism, still stretched our imaginations to the maximum to picture eventual Communism, still have referred to bourgeois values, the class struggle, the rôle of the workers, the necessity for Party discipline. And if we had talked for long, we would still have thought about Tolstoy and Heine and Shelley and Balzac. When you were in hiding and you joined that theatrical touring company, you came to Anygyalföld – did you ever recall it? – and I found you rehearsing in a warehouse, but you had a small part and you were sitting on a crate bent double like a jack-knife over a book, and the book was Lukács' on Drama. We would still have said that that was the way to live, theory and practice inseparable. But during those thirty years we also changed. Our words had had to get different jobs done. Even the name of Budapest changed its meaning – as it will always change. I mean, however, for us two personally. For me Budapest is largely what I left. For you it was perhaps what you found when you returned there with the Red Army a few years ago. And so with every other word. We both had to defend ourselves during those thirty years against different threats. And so we must have become eagle-eyed about, wary of, different factors.

Four o'clock in the morning has just struck and the sky through the skylight lifts up. It is dawn: the dawn we always used as the image of the future – the one cliché which is indestructible; the dawn we so often had reason to fear; the dawn under which your control of your own weight collapsed and you fell dead, roots meaningless in the air like a tree's. Forgive my words, Laci. You knew the danger of them. But I must see it in detail. When I watch a London bus gently, slowly moving along the traffic-laden street, I must see the instantaneous completeness of your collapse, and in the faces of the crowd on the sidewalk I must see the blank eyes of the militia as they lower their rifles. I must because I cannot see otherwise.

We did not, of course, through those thirty years, which really constituted our life, face totally different threats. The vast sequence of history was the same for us both. But we understand that. We never addressed lectures to one another. Do not let us begin now. The differences that developed in our lives only revealed themselves in where we chose to flatten ourselves against the wall as the great, necessary simplifications roared past us, or in how we thought when we were clinging on to them. Now the massive answers to the question roar past. You were a traitor; it is the hardest thing in the world to be a Communist, and eventually you yielded, you failed: you were a traitor. You were innocent; the dictatorship of the proletariat has become a police state; the revolution has been betrayed; you were innocent. But after these have passed, there remains, small as the pain is sharp, your confession and my doubt. And these are the result of our different lives, your different death.

I must go to bed. But I have not finished. I shall never finish. That is my guilt to which I confess. I have made myself doubly an *emigré*. I have not returned to our country. And I have chosen to spend my life on my art, instead of on immediate objectives. Thus I am a spectator watching what I might have participated in. Thus I question endlessly. Thus I risk reducing the world within my own mind to my own dimensions for the sake of discovering a small truth that has remained undiscovered by others. It may be that we have both betrayed that fourth man we were waiting on. I must sleep to work. Work can be finished. Forgive.

NOVEMBER 28

Drew all day for the Lido. Is it possible to paint a picture today as happy as a Veronese? Therein is the dreadful obliqueness of art. I am miserable, haunted by Laszlo and my own helplessness, and yet painstakingly and not as a consolation, I am planning a canvas which shall celebrate holiday pleasure. This obliqueness is what enrages most planners. Veronese was summoned by the Inquisition to explain why he painted a dog instead of Mary Magdalene. But the artist's obliqueness is not entirely arbitrary. Laszlo wanted poems and novels to be written about the Party and the new steel plants – and then obliquely fell to becoming traitor or martyr. And now I, unable to forget Laszlo and the loathsome price paid for my own better fortune, nevertheless begin to paint a canvas of popular celebration. Art can turn corners so much more rapidly than Policy. Use it as a ferret, not as a four for pulling the State Coach – nobler as the second rôle sounds.

NOVEMBER 30
Two days later the last sentence shocks me. We must never, never make a virtue of our lonely burrowing. It has already led to too many perversions.

DECEMBER 7
The Ministry Inspectors came round the School today. Peering like giraffes down at every drawing-board. Hardwick followed them, rubbing his hands.

'Mr Lavin is our link with tradition,' he explained. And I thought: yes, I who was painting abstract paintings when you were five years old.

DECEMBER 12
Today I said 'no' three times, and spent most of the day thinking why, and then looking at the Lido canvas. It is 2 metres high, but it should be 4.

First, Hancock phoned up. He did want to commission a painting. Would I paint his wife, he said. Jokingly I replied that perhaps she wouldn't want to pose. That's the trouble, he said, but I'm sure you could persuade her. The way he said this puzzled me. I asked him what he meant. And then after much going round the point, he explained that he wanted me to paint a nude of her. I said 'No', that was impossible, she wouldn't ever agree, and he should paint her himself. I could not help laughing, but he took it very seriously.

The second time was to Max. He asked me to guarantee his fare to America. He had some improbable story about how in the old days he had met a man who had asked him to turn a rival's wedding into a farce, and how he, Max, had laid a trail of aniseed and let a pack of dogs into the church, and how this man now had a restaurant in California and wanted Max to go out there and manage the cabaret. When I told him I didn't believe it, he admitted it wasn't true, and said that the real trouble was that Barbara had left him. This must be the tenth time. I replied categorically. I haven't the money, anyway. But even if I had

had it, I would refuse. And I told him so. America for him is only another patch in his no-man's-land. He would leave with neither regret nor hatred, but only with added pride at having 'alienated' himself once more. America would merely become the new backdrop to his monologue which would be just that much fuller of self-pity. I asked him why he didn't go back to Germany. He made the excuse that Barbara wouldn't like it. But that confirmed my suspicions that he hoped to persuade Barbara to go with him to America. If he can, he will take her there as you take a gramophone for when the nights are too quiet even to dream. Max can make me angrier than any man I know.

The third time was to a journalist from *News*. He had interviewed George Trent as a young British painter. And George sent him to me – as the artist who had taught him most! His first question over the phone put me on my guard. Was I Janos Lavin, the *Hungarian* painter, and could he come round and take some photographs and interview me? I asked him what he wanted to question me about. Your work, why you chose to work in the Free World, your opinion about the present state of art in Hungary, etc. No, I said, I had nothing to tell him.

Depressed as I am tonight, these three trivial incidents – or, rather, my reaction to them – seem to sum up the circumstances of my present life. In each case I reacted negatively. I have set myself outside all opportunity. All that it is possible for me to do is to cover that white canvas which is too small and when it is finished put it against the wall behind the others. Such a limit is grief. And there is no guile to grief. I work because I can do nothing else. Katinka, Laci, Ernö, Yvonne with your maiden hair like parsley, Walther, Susie – you lived.

1953

JANUARY 6

My friend, the old man down the road, has died. The last time I spoke to him he said, 'I've been thinking. You know there are only three men who are necessary, the farmer, the fisherman and the miner. The rest are parasites.'

Another death. I realize that I am now painting in the same

spirit as other men make their wills. And like them I want my wishes to be absolutely clear.

JANUARY 14

Behind the figures in the Lido are white tiles, with a barely perceptible pink behind their glaze – Indian red giving the white not so much a colour as an edge, to cut the turquoise water below. On the tiles is a large design of swimmers in blue outline. The juxtaposition within a painting of art and life is one that interests me greatly: the relationship, I mean, between the design of bathers on the tiles and the bathers themselves. It was a surrealist device at one stage. But it need not be. On a quite different level, it resembles the use of mirrors in their paintings by the Dutch interiorists. It is also not so far removed from Veronese's use of *trompe l'œil* in his frescoes.

JANUARY 20

Hardwick called me into his office and told me that my life-drawing class was to be merged with Evans's. He repeatedly said that he hoped I understood that it was entirely a question of another room being needed for lithography. He said this so often that I knew it wasn't the reason. He is preparing for the cuts in staff that may be necessary. When they come, a few will be seen to be dispensable. The loss of the money will be serious enough. But what disgusts me is the attitude of the staff themselves. Nothing is said. Everyone looks the other way. And then secretly and in turn they all go up to Hardwick and either talk about their latest sale, their coming exhibition or else discuss how worried they are about such-and-such a student – this last to impress on Hardwick how keenly they feel their job. Thus – jealousy. Thus in their work the desperate attempt to find some little trick of their own. The circus and the variety theatre – whom we resemble so closely – have a hundred times more solidarity.

FEBRUARY 1

I seek in the juxtaposition of the bathers and the outlines on the tiles – a sense of tenderness. There is the formal excitement: the contrast between the bare, empty blue outlines and the outlines of the actual figures only just resisting the pressure of the colour they contain; the contrast between the movement that is resolved and the movement that is just becoming. In the formal sense the drawing on the tiles is like a mask or a cast from which the actual figures have broken free. But all this is only my means for expressing the vulnerability of my figures, for as soon as one recognizes vulnerability, which is so different from weakness or the tragic, one experiences a sense of tenderness. Without tenderness, pleasure means nothing. You need only look at animals to see the truth of that. It is gentleness that distinguishes their playing from the actions they constantly take to ensure their survival. My difficulty is to express this pleasure, this tenderness or gentleness, whilst keeping the figures anonymous. And how little that word is understood now. To seek the anonymous is thought to be inhuman. But it is in the anonymous that we discover what we all share and therefore what is profoundly human. In the shape of a foreshortened thigh, in two eyes, their lids lifted, looking, I paint my requiem for Laszlo, who was executed, in a far truer manner than if I attempted a portrait of him as I remember him. And in my four figures, naked for pleasure, I paint what he died for – if he died for anything.

FEBRUARY 7

My particular misery is that I can only think of Laszlo in terms of the past. Revolutionary discipline depends on the individual conscience. That is not theoretical idealism! It is practical intelligence. After the revolution you can grow by exterior discipline imposed by revolutionary soldiers and courts, or self-imposed by individual revolutionaries who suppress the promptings of their own consciences for the sake of unity, or as the result of their respect for the intelligence of their leaders. But before the revolution, when the arrests are being made and the confessions extorted, the only thing that stands between the revolutionary movement and its betrayal is the individual conscience. What stops a man informing under torture is his knowledge that, if he gives way, the rest of his life will be even more terrible for him to bear than the pain he now suffers. He is at that moment beyond not only the aid but also the praise or contempt of his comrades. Solidarity, loyalty, his vision of his comrades whom he will not betray, become then only the *image* that his personal conscience can hold to and express itself by. Of the revolutionaries I have known, those who have suffered most have been the most obstinate. Their obstinacy has been like the hard tissue of the healed flesh beneath their scars. It has been the condition of their survival, and they cannot lose it. Sometimes their obstinacy has shown itself in their apparently unquestioning support of everything the Party has done. But even in their cases it is conceivable – such is the history and quality of their obstinacy – that one day it might be turned against some decision of the Central Committee. Laszlo was such a man.

Simply: those who have lived through some extreme suffering and danger see their lives whole. They have watched their own lives as you can watch a shooting-star. It is impossible for them to live at the beck and call of vague generalizations. They know too well how much depends on particulars – the particular wrong answer, the particular bowl of soup, the strength of a particular pair of lungs. They know their own particulars – in every sense. They know exactly what they can give to the movement. They want to give it all. But they also know that this cannot be an automatic all. They have discovered that their will is stronger than outside arguments. Historical necessity does not of itself make heroes; but the realization of historical necessity can make heroes. Laszlo was such a man.

Those who consolidate a revolution are sometimes men of a different sort. Their leaders may be old revolutionaries. But they themselves – the functionaries, the police officers, the local officials – they perhaps have never had their consciences tested. They are faced with the obstinacy of the old bourgeoisie who do not wish to cooperate. They may face the ruthlessness of active counter-revolutionaries. To them it may seem that Socialism is being attacked by countless recalcitrant individuals. They come to fear spontaneity. Yet all revolutions in history have been partly spontaneous. Above all, they fear the protestant conscience – the phenomenon which once stood between their party and its betrayal. Was it in this way that Laszlo was found guilty by his heirs?

FEBRUARY 13

Blue separates: arms always wide apart holding off the other, combatant colours.

FEBRUARY 21

Have worked for a week on the Lido. If only I didn't have to finish it.

FEBRUARY 26

My dear Diana, You are now asleep. You use even sleep as a weapon, as a comment on the constant disappointment you suffer whilst awake. If you could snore, you would – to push the lesson home.

I look round this garage of a studio. We have lived in it for nearly twenty years – another fact in your armoury.

Tonight we quarrelled about the coffee-pot – what an excuse! Does the humiliation of it ever strike you? As you settle down afterwards to write letters to your relatives and friends. And is that also a designed comment, because I never write letters to where I once belonged?

I have been to look at you. You are asleep, but not quite as I imagined. Your mouth is slightly open – unkissed and wordless. Your hand is loose on the pillow, as if it were holding an invisible sheaf of papers. Our histories maybe.

We quarrel about coffee-pots or politics. But that is only because we cannot quarrel about what separates us. Once we did – a hundred years ago.

You lie like a knight in his armour. That is not a woman's way of lying. It is terrible. But it is impressive. You wanted to fight, but because the fight never existed and so could never be won or lost, you now have to fight all the time. It is a bad habit, but if I sit back very calmly, I know that it is not the worst of bad habits. You are hateful, Rosie. But in those four words, in defiance of our protests, we admit – what? – that you are still asleep, still only ten yards away.

You wanted to fight. But you also wanted to see the outcome. Whereas in my struggle you never can. And so you deduced 'no outcome' means 'failure'. And you put your lipstick on in the morning more carefully to hide it. And you searched in your bitter disappointment – keeping your questioning eyes away from me because you knew I wouldn't give you an answer – you searched for the cause. And you found my politics. You accuse me of my politics. But, believe me, if I were politically involved you could then have had your fight – beside me and beside thousands of others whose greatest virtue is that they have no sense of failure, who, on the contrary, have an unshakeable belief in their continuing success. No, the Communist in me is our scapegoat. The enemy is the artist, with his inconclusive one-man struggle. And you are right, you being you: he is the enemy. And in this you are in agreement with the Communist leaders you so ignorantly and maliciously libel.

Yet I deceived you. I have thought often that I met you and fell in love with you as a soldier with a nurse in a hospital. And under those conditions all the gentleness of the nurse – and if she too falls in love, as you did, Rosie – all the idealistic part of her love, are diverted towards making the soldier fighting fit again. But I never went back to the front. To any front that you could recognize as such. I slipped away to paint. That is how I deceived you and disillusioned you. You didn't see what it meant at first. You thought you could fight in this new arena as in any other. And so one can, in fact. Take any young artist who is talented and hopeful and who later becomes renowned, repetitive and hollow, and in nine cases out of ten you will find a scheming, fighting ambitious wife in the centre of the story. They promote to ruin, these women. Yet even now you will think I am making excuses.

Never mind. It is our qualities not our defects that separate us. Your loyalty – for the last thing you will do is to abandon me to my 'failure', and my refusal to compromise. From these qualities arise our pettiness. Your jealousies, your need for the political scapegoat, your cherished cultivation of your own disappointment. My suspiciousness. My selfish austerity. My discontent.

Why cannot we talk with the honesty with which I am now writing? Because the last quarrel is never over. Our disappointment is never completed. And so is not complete. My hell of a Rosie.

Your loyalty weighs me down. You hate my determination.

We have turned each other's qualities sour. But because we know that originally they were qualities, we do not leave each other.

Or that at least is part of the truth. There is also another truth. You pay for this studio out of your money, and you also earn a few pounds a week out of that damned library you file in. What I earn goes towards materials and a few extras. We are used to it now, and we never mention it. Nor have we ever quarrelled about this. This, the simple economic basis of our life, is the subject of our most guarded secrets – which, nevertheless, we both know. Your secret is that you do not believe in the work I am able to do as a result of my dependence on you. My secret is that I know this. If we told our secrets, we would have to stop. It is hard at our age to break our habits.

Do you know, Rosie, if I could I would earn £500 tomorrow and we would go to Italy for six months? You should have your holiday. You should get brown again. If there was anything I could do to make that possible, I would do it. But if I told you that, you would make yourself ugly and say, 'Do you take me for a fool?' You cannot believe it because you cannot see that the painter has been reduced to a menial. You would believe it if an unskilled worker said it, but you do not see that a painter is in the same position. The worker has a hope – if his football pools turn up. The painter has a hope – if a fashion turns up.

Do you remember after the war when they published my book of drawings? That was the nearest my luck got us. And in those days you used to creep up behind me whilst I was working at the easel and waggle a hand in front of my face and laugh. If you knew how often I've thought of that, and how often I have since longed to be interrupted by a silly, waggling hand, you would know that if it were a question of choice, I would choose.

But how remote this letter is! How tender compared to our life! That is why I write it for myself in Hungarian, sign it for myself. Address it for myself. You unhappy dragging bitch. You Rosie I have made.

MARCH 25

Stalin is dead. Dead as Laszlo. Laszlo's death was the end of a comradeship. Whichever way I resolve my doubts, it comes to that. In Moscow there is a queue, several miles long, filing past to see the Marshal lying in state. Laszlo was thrown somewhere. Last night I dreamt I was taken to a remote building in a deserted part of some country. When I stepped out of the car, I had to climb up a long steep shingle beach to the building. There was a strange sharp smell in the air. Then an official came out of the building, and told me that the crystal-like pebbles which I was walking on and which made the going so hard were all fragments of human bones. Yet all I did was to stop and take off one of my shoes to shake out two sharp fragments that were hurting my foot. Such is our attitude to death itself. It is the man's life that obsesses us after he is dead. Were you? You died knowing for certain that you were either guilty or innocent. How did Stalin die? How did this man whose name was a promise all over the world, an assurance that revolutions could succeed, how did this man meet his own private death? Even the B.B.C. announced the news with solemnity. The whole world was waiting for him to die, and, momentarily, all mourn his greatness now that it is dispensable. Many also mourn in his death, those who died at Stalingrad, those whose unrecorded lives were snuffed out in Europe, those who must die in Asia and Africa without doctors either to cure or to plot.

AUGUST 6

It is months since I have written in this book. I have only worked.

Janos said to me once, 'This working, it is always the same. At nine o'clock in the morning you are full of plans and ability and the truth. At four o'clock in the afternoon you are a failure.'

I have painted two nudes. Although nobody may know it, the nude is a revolutionary subject. The body suggests, on a sensuous level, all that man is capable of becoming on every level when he has at last created that society which will be worthy of himself. On the back of a box of matches I bought the other day, is a joke: 'Time: the stuff between pay days.' Such exactly is the squalor of consciousness capitalism has brought to so many who live under it.

85

What sort of time would you have bought Laci on that last morning? Any time. But that doesn't alter the truth of what I've just written.

Everything between the bone and the surface of the flesh, all that part of the body in which sensations dart like angel fish or pain bites like a shark, must be created by colour.

AUGUST 10

Began re-working one of the nudes.

The leaves of a chestnut tree in a summer light and a summer wind. Each leaf moves to disclose another and another. It is like shuffling a pack of cards. But each card is a slightly different green. It would be much easier to paint it in red than green.

AUGUST 11

Spent the evening with the Hancocks. I am always surprised by Len. He once said that the artist is the happiest man alive. He is one of the happiest men I have ever known.

The affair of the nude of Mrs Hancock remained a constant source of amusement. One morning about this time I remember Len coming round to the studio to deliver a frame that a carpenter friend of his had made for Janos.

'How about that painting of your beautiful wife? Have you begun on it?' Janos asked him.

'It's no joke, I can tell you,' said Len, trying to peer at the canvas Janos was working on.

'I did not mean it as a joke. I was being serious.'

'Come off it. How can I paint her? It's got to be a professional job. I couldn't do her justice, Janos. And she knows it.'

Janos said nothing from behind his canvas, and Len walked about before speaking again.

'I mentioned to her my idea that you should paint her.'

'And?'

'She blew her top.'

'What?'

'She was furious.'

'That is what I told you.' Janos chuckled. 'You cannot ask your

wife to pose for other men. The other men, they must ask her.'

'But you're a professional. Not just any Tom, Dick or Harry. A nude's a common or garden thing for you. Part of your trade' – he paused, at a loss for words to describe how simply he saw the situation – 'like meat's mine.'

He stopped walking about and addressed the back of the large canvas.

'Anyway, if that's what you think, why can't you ask her?'

Janos appeared round the side of the canvas, trying to keep a straight face.

'It is too late now. You have told her and she would rightly think it a plot. If you want to have a painting of her, you must paint it yourself. Anyway, if all men painted their wives there would be more beautiful wives. That is certain.'

'If I started it, would you touch it up for me?'

At this Janos laughed outright, and continued laughing, his temples going rosy beneath his tufty hair.

'Man. Paint her yourself. Or put the idea out of your head.'

And he went back behind his easel, and was still laughing when Len left.

AUGUST 12

I have an idea to paint girls on roller-skates. I have made an etching of it. But for a painting, the subject seems too particular, my vision of it too momentary.

AUGUST 13

The girls on roller-skates remind me. When Laszlo was about eight years old he had a fight with an enemy of ours. They fought round a pump. Laszlo, running round it, pulled the pump handle down as he ran. The handle came up under his pursuer's chin and knocked three of his teeth out. The boy fled howling. Later Laszlo's father heard about it and beat Laszlo. After his beating, furious, he found me. 'He knocked his own teeth out,' he said. 'He knocked his own teeth out!'

AUGUST 14

I am working on a small canvas of a man with a ladder. The shape of the rungs of the ladder is almost as subtle as limbs.

The more I understand of myself and the more I understand of the temperament of those artists whom I admire, the more I am convinced that what separates talent from genius is nothing more nor less than confidence: the ability not to be frightened of making a fool of yourself. This is a dangerous thing to say. It opens the door to sheer bravura. But that is a very different thing from the kind of confidence I am talking about. Bravura comes from the desire to impress which in turn comes from the same fear of making a fool of yourself. The confidence I speak of is not made out of the opinions of others. It comes from solitude, which is the condition of our working; it comes from our realizing that our primary duty is to our capabilities. How those capabilities can best be used depends upon the social situation. I offer no excuse for standing aloof from the struggles of our time: for the painter to paint still lives when other men are being killed in the street. I do not even offer an excuse for myself, a passive spectator of Laszlo's death – whether his ultimate executioners live in Moscow or the Pentagon. Our capabilities are not constant and absolute – a violinist of genius does not automatically fulfil all his capabilities by playing his violin on every occasion; our capabilities are simply the means by which we can use for the maximum social good the particular situation we find ourselves in. The greatest violinist cannot be justified in playing his violin on the bank of a river in which a drowning man is shouting for help. But at the same time if we deny, doubt, hide from ourselves, exaggerate, disguise or do anything but accept our own capabilities, we become half-men, sophisticates, cynics, time-servers. Such half-men abound in this society, for it is a society incapable of recognizing or using the capabilities of the vast majority of its citizens. 'Capitalism violates the world as a senile old man violates a young healthy woman whom he is impotent to impregnate with anything besides the disease of senility.' The recognition of every man's capabilities should be an exterior social process; it has become a personal and introspective one which only a few have the strength to even partially carry through.

The dilemma of the artist is unimportant, if you are considering his art. But it can be important if you consider it as an intense reflection of a wider but less obvious dilemma. If we are to continue working at all under capitalism, only two possible attitudes of mind are open to us: we must be either ambitious or arrogant. The humble artist is a man whom we shall only re-discover much later. Today the artist either serves or searches arrogantly alone. Few, of course, of those who serve do so consciously. Simply, they are more frightened of making fools of themselves than they are aware of their true capabilities. The power of fashion is based on the fear of being a fool. The ambitious artist is the man who places his talent on the pedestal of good opinion. And how we all long to be in such a position! There is nothing essentially shameful in it. But everything depends upon the state of contemporary opinion. There are fish that you throw back into the sea as not being worth the catch. And there – in that last sentence – is the other attitude of mind: the arrogant attitude.

Bill Neale would say this was a false dilemma that could only be posed by a bourgeois artist frightened of the people. Serve *them*, I can hear him saying, and you'll purge yourself of both ambition and arrogance. But he is wrong. It is in the name and the virtue and the potentiality of the life that the working class can gain for the world, that I am arrogant. All their strength, of which many of them are yet unaware, is reflected in my *naïveté*.

I worked all day on *The Ladder*.

AUGUST 26
What faces peer through the paper at me. I work like an actor on a stage.

SEPTEMBER 2
This morning was restless, and so I walked, down into Ken-sington High Street and then to Knightsbridge. Thinking. As part of the business of everything being made a commodity, the shop window has taken the place of the altar-piece and the painting. Tens of thousands look into these windows and wonder. Here are the modern still-lives and the modern heroes and heroines. The function of the shop-window tableau is really the same as that of sculpture for the Greeks, or frescoes for the Italians of the Renaissance. These works appealed because

they embodied the hopes, the ideals, the potentiality of most of the people who looked at them. Today there is only one common ideal, created and fostered by commerce: it is the principle that *Only what you haven't yet got is worth having.* The shop window is the living expression of this ideal. The dreams dreamt in front of shop windows begin in the same way (although they do not reach the same end) as the dreams dreamt in front of a work by Phidias.

Which again reminds me. Laszlo was on his way to school in the morning. He passed a tailor's shop with a window broken by rioters. The street was deserted and in the front of the window was a pair of boy's long trousers on a dummy. For months he had been plaguing his mother to let him have a pair of long trousers. No, she said, he'd be old enough to have trousers when he was old enough to earn his living, not before. He hesitated in front of the shop. No one was in sight. His father always said the shopkeepers robbed the people, so why shouldn't he rob a shopkeeper?

He stood there undecided, also wondering how quickly he could take the trousers off the dummy. He walked on. Then he stopped. Walked back. Wondered. Walked on, still arguing with himself. At that moment another boy, older than he, came running down the street towards him. As this other boy passed the shop he seized the whole dummy, trousers and all, and ran on with the legs stuck under his arm. Laszlo ran after him, shouting Robber! Thief! The boy took no notice and as he ran he unbuttoned the trousers and slipped them off the plaster legs. When the trousers were off, he threw the legs behind him at Laszlo. They broke on the cobbles, and Laszlo stopped whilst the boy ran on out of sight. Soon Laszlo heard footsteps from the opposite direction, and took to his heels. 'I felt very guilty,' he said when he had finished telling me the story. 'As if I *had* stolen them myself.' Most confessions exaggerate, as if the exaggeration could amend.

SEPTEMBER 10

This morning was fine after days of rain. I walked as far as Battersea bridge. It was a slightly yellow autumn light, beginning to become opaque. There are days when London becomes tangible and today was one of them. You feel then that the scale of London is only a question of the repetition of the corners you can see round, roofs whose angles you can judge, streets that you can continue to cross and walk down, buildings that rise up four square on their foundations and are encompassable, trees that grow upward where stone has left a place for them; the mystery of London vanishes; it ceases to be a dumb force; it becomes a city built and inhabited by men. Paris always seems to be this, Berlin less often, London only rarely. I hate the ghosts of London, but on days like this they are laid, and the elderberry bush just outside my studio window is no longer the limit of the intelligible environment, but a plain natural object that roughly marks where my activities end and those of other men begin. I bought Diana a green leather belt. She was delighted. Finished *The Ladder*.

SEPTEMBER 14

I have been looking through an old international catalogue of sculpture and came across some reproductions of Gonzalez. He had the face of a count and the voice of a sincere priest, but he was a prodigious metal-worker. I still believe that *La Montserrat* is one of the few great sculptures of this century. Today it is a lonely work lost in the modern museums of artefacts. Yet if I had made that, as Julio did, I would be content. Drew in Covent Garden most of the day and came back very cold.

SEPTEMBER 15

Worked badly. It began with my upsetting a whole bag of cadmium yellow when mixing some with the oil. I need a holiday. I scooped it up like pollen – the yellow of the Alföld.

Why does this yellow remind me of Laszlo's medical? The fact is that he is never out of my mind. We were called up then when we were seventeen. We used to watch the country boys come into the city for their examinations, each carrying a little wooden box with his belongings in it. If we could get talking to any of them, we always told them to go to the doctor without their box: the box suggested that they themselves thought they were fit enough. And if they were really bright, we told them some of the dodges they could try – excessive coffee to make your pulse race, various herbs to make you vomit, soap up your penis to produce the symptoms of gonorrhoea. We saved a good number.

Laci himself pretended to be deaf, demanding that everything should be written on a piece of paper for him. Leonard Gough often reminds me of that. The doctor ordered him to sit on one side – he would be examined later. In order not to betray any reaction to what he heard he sat on a bench and imagined he was watching a mouse on the floor. He watched the imaginary mouse all the morning. Occasionally the doctor gave him a suspicious glance and whispered something to the sergeant standing at his side. He was kept sitting on that bench all day. After the last conscript had been examined, the doctor smiled at him and said benignly, All right you can go. Laci continued to watch the mouse, without the slightest sign of having understood. He had survived the trick. The sergeant came up to him and literally kicked him out of the door. Or at least that was Laci's story. How simple the methods of interrogation were then. All you needed was an imaginary mouse.

SEPTEMBER 17

Met Max for a drink. He has got a small job in a film, but is very pessimistic about it. His lazy sense of failure is the result of a kind of false and terrible perfectionism. Nothing can ever be like Berlin was. Nobody can ever appreciate him as he was appreciated then. And so everything that happens now is absurd, and he performs with one hand in his pocket. He said I was too proud with Diana: that she longs to console me and I never let her. Console? I always leave Max with the feeling that either he is mad or that I am living in a fool's paradise. For what do I need consolation?

MARGATE – SEPTEMBER 20

I spent the whole morning on the rocks near the North Foreland lighthouse. Diana is with friends at Glyndebourne Opera, and will be here in two days. I could not go with her, for the audience there enrages me too much. All art is meaningless to those for whom life itself is only a spectacle.

The sound of the sea is the oldest in the world, and to walk along the wrack-line is as humbling, as belittling, as watching from an astronomer's observatory. You are confronted in the same way with a scale with which you cannot grapple. On one rock there may be ten thousand mussels.

On a promontory of rock I watched the tide come in round me. In the gulleys between the rocks you could see the white froth lolloping in towards the cliffs, just the top of the white froth, so that each wave looked as if it had released a score of white rabbits which, hidden in the gulleys except for their absurd white tails, bounded towards the cliffs. The sea was the turgid, muddy colour of shrimps before they are boiled; the sky the colour of a galvanized bucket that has lost its shine. Like no European seascape that I have seen painted. More Chinese.

Watching the water I thought of the banks of the Tisza. I used to stare, fascinated, at the cracks and fissures in the dried clay, imagining earthquakes and wondering how it would feel if the earth suddenly opened under my feet. All imagination first begins in fear. But how few realize today that this is only its starting-off point! Spontaneity and intuition are used as excuses for never making the hard, necessary journey from that first point.

It was on the banks of the Tisza that Laszlo and I made love to our first girls. The evenings on Margaret Island with the gigantic flow of the Danube emphasizing how accurately ten small fingers can interlock and then go courting to release passion that mocks even the depth of the river – but those evenings were later when Laci read his poems at the *Ma* meetings and we knew we were tomorrow's heroes! On the Tisza we were less sure of ourselves. Or Laci was, anyway. He brought a girl whom he had met in Pest at some students' meeting. Her name was Juli. She must have been about eighteen, a year or two older than him: a magnificent girl with black hair, olive skin and very open eyes that showed off her temperament for all to see. She was the daughter of a rich bourgeois family who lived in one of the city hotels. She wore an expensive bracelet and obviously tailored clothes; yet none of this hid the impressive coarse energy with which she pushed herself to the front of whatever was happening, not out of greed but out of sheer zest. Only

93

when Laszlo was talking was she quiet and unobtrusive. Whether she was really interested in what he was saying, I don't know. But as we walked along or sat at a café table, Laszlo explained the future to us, quoted Ady, described what Paris would be like when we discovered it and told Pest stories. He talked very intensely, emotions passing over his long face one after another whilst his hands gathered new ones from the air. Juli looked up at him, with submissive eyes, and was restrained as a horse between shafts until he stopped talking. That evening they went off together, arms round one another's backs. He began to kiss her. Some herons flew overhead and landed near the river. They sat down on the grass to watch them, and immediately they were in each other's arms. Laci, murmuring, as I can imagine, poetic phrases, began to caress her interminably. After about half an hour Juli, disengaging herself, said, 'Look! I despise half measures'; and then, flinging her arms out sideways on to the ground, lay on her back. Shamed by his diffidence, he instantly fell on top of her, but once there, fumbling with skirts and trousers and petticoats, he still hesitated. She pulled his head down, 'Baba, do I have to wait nine months for you, too?' Thus, Laszlo lost his virginity and came back to the village prouder. They also both came back with their hair lank and black and wet, for they had bathed between times. Two months later we heard that Juli had married a banker's son. They fled the country in 1919. No more is known. We were a generation of unfinished stories. But we did tell them to one another.

SEPTEMBER 22

Diana arrived today. She looked much rested. I did a drawing of her. If only we could live as clearly as I can draw.

SEPTEMBER 23

Last night we had supper on the pier and we danced. There comes a time when you enjoy simply watching and observing the happiness of others – sensuously enjoy I mean. This enjoyment comes from the knowledge once gained from your own pleasures but is now quite disinterested. I enjoyed seeing a youth daring, as he danced, to touch the girl's hair with his lips as she turned

94

her head away. Age can bring this time about. But so does the practice of art – prematurely.

SEPTEMBER 25

The English landscape is fantastic. If I had been born here, I might have been able to paint it. But it would mean approaching painting from exactly the opposite direction from which I do. It is essentially an *unfixed*, mysterious, romantic landscape. Nothing is disclosed. Other landscapes lie naked to the eye: but what you see of the English landscape is like a garment on a torso that is constantly moving; in fact, it is the light that moves, but the effect is like a green shirt worn by a swordsman duelling with an invisible figure in the sky. Pure romance.

SEPTEMBER 26

We sat on the rocks, throwing pebbles into the water.

I like the sea, she said, Look! Do you think that's a boat out there or a buoy?

A buoy.

How old were you when you first saw the sea?

It was in Belgium. I must have been about thirty.

How funny. It's one of the first things I can ever remember.

Would you like to live by the sea? I asked her.

Yes. No. But I'd like to go on a cruise. To India and back on a cargo-boat or something.

You could, if you wanted to.

And you?

I would be all right.

She frowned. I didn't mean that. Wouldn't you come?

It would cost double.

Yes. But forgetting the money. Wouldn't you come?

When I've finished the next big canvas.

There's always the next big canvas.

She sighed and was silent for several minutes.

It wasn't a buoy, she said, it was a fishing-boat.

SEPTEMBER 28

Coming back, after a week, to the studio, how impatient I am to begin working again. After only a week, it looks like a closed-down factory. You can feel the air of unemployment. *The Waves* are good. The nude I re-worked is terrible – overpainted. *The Ladder* is the beginning of something. But it is only a part, a detail.

OCTOBER 12

Worked all day on an idea for a head. I can settle to nothing big at the moment. But I worked hard, building all day. Tomorrow it will be just another small canvas which is no more than an exercise. Later it will temporarily become a commodity that nobody wants. One day it may or may not be 'very interesting as an example of . . .' Tonight it is perfect: a day's work.

OCTOBER 13

I drank too much wine last night when I wrote that.

OCTOBER 24

Ever since I saw the Olympic Games in 1948 I have wanted to paint them. At the time I filled a book with drawings, but I could never feel what I wanted as a whole. Now the idea is coming up again and I have a glimmering. It was one of the purest experiences of my life: thousands of people with tears in their eyes, which were tears of pure disinterested admiration. 'Zatopek! Zatopek!' they shouted as though he were the son of them all. Just played with paint today to remind myself that it's only coloured shit.

NOVEMBER 5

I have begun a portrait of John. Just drawings so far. It is difficult to get his suspiciousness. Always a bit like a bird breaking a snail on a stone.

It was Janos's idea to do the portrait. He had often said he would, and now, I think, he welcomed the prospect of having company in the studio for a few hours a week. (That Janos never talked to me about Laszlo's execution now shocks me profoundly. We were friends and we were political comrades, but he could not trust me. Clearly there was no one to whom I could or would betray him. But I do not mean trust in that sense. He could not trust that I would not add in some way to his predicament and shame.) *We conversed spasmodically. He talked mostly either about his past or about his plans for the future – including his idea of painting the Olympic Games.*

Whilst he was working his expression was comparatively relaxed. It was when he stopped, lit a cigarette or went across to the cupboard to find another pen that his face looked tired. And then, as if he wanted a subject to distract him, he would sometimes say something like: 'Why did you say Rembrandt was the first modern artist?' or – in a quite different vein – 'Do you like this new Monroe film star?' 'Marilyn?' 'Yes. The one with the vast breasts.' But he would say this, turning away and looking absently at the blackened elder bush outside the window.

NOVEMBER 13

Have done two drawings of J. that I like. I have now postponed having my lunch till three o'clock. This way I feel less guilty sleeping after I have eaten.

As Janos looked at me I looked at him. When it was cold he wore an old short leather coat, like a roadsweeper's, and this made it seem incongruous that he should be sitting crosslegged on a chair working intently with a fine pen in a small book. When he stopped to rake out the studio stove and put some more coke in it, one had the impression that these movements were far more natural to him. Only if one stood above him, looking down at his long hand actually drawing, did one remember that energy need have nothing to do with scale.

After numerous drawings, he did a small oil sketch of just my head. He worked on this far more feverishly than on the drawings, constantly swearing, stepping back from the canvas, looking at it in the mirror and stepping round to look at me from different angles.

Every half hour or so, he would lift the small easel to the other end of the studio, and we would stare at it from a distance together, and smoke a cigarette. To my eye it progressed well and steadily. But not to his. Every time we stopped he was dissatisfied with another small passage of the painting. He squinted at it, put up his long, brown hand to shield off part of it from his vision, pursed his lips, put up his hand again to shield off another part, swore, hesitated, then took a brush from his hand, loaded it with paint from the paint table and strode down the studio to make an alteration. Often when he stepped back, I could see no difference; but to him it was always either better or worse.

Thus we went on for four days. Sometimes he scraped an area down to the canvas again. Several times he radically changed the colour of the background. When he had it as he wanted it, he said: 'Look. You see. That ear. It begins to belong now.' After we had finished for the day, he would turn the canvas to the wall and say, 'At last. Enough.' But after we had been talking for half an hour or so, he would get up in the middle of saying something and go over to turn the canvas round and look at it, without interrupting his sentence.

This nervousness and hesitation struck me because I had never suspected that Janos would work in such a way – even with a portrait. His final works were so simple, flat and assured that I had overestimated the straightforwardness of his confidence.

When the sketch was finished, he said: 'Now for the portrait. I like this because it's like you, but it is no painting.'

NOVEMBER 27

Have worked for three days on the portrait without J. It is better like this. You should be able to paint a recognizable portrait if you know the sitter with his eyes blindfolded. Colour and form must make the expression of the character. The expression on the face is only a sign – like a weathercock. All temperament can lie between red and blue.

I came to the studio one morning, and there was the portrait on the canvas, already half finished. The morning was foggy and barely light so that the bright, very definite colours on the canvas looked as artificial as the colours of tinned food. Janos worked all the morning under the fluorescent light. This was possible because he used only the limited number of colours he had mixed into piles on his palette the day before when the light was good enough to judge their values by. The fog filtered into the studio until finally it was impossible to go on any more. Instead we sat either side of the stove and talked. 'It is odd to think that the Impressionists would have found this exciting,' he said, referring to the fog, and then suddenly *and vehemently, 'It is this that makes me feel most a foreigner. I hate it so much.'*

'So do we.'

'Yes. But you differently. You endure it. I rage against it – like it was an injustice, like something that's been done to my eyes by the English. Still I feel that.' And he laughed wryly at himself. Then he began to talk about how when he was younger he used sometimes to lose his temper with his paintings and destroy them. 'A little I understand the brutal murderer. After the first blow it is easy. You destroy to destroy your blow before – till there is not anything left. Even one time I have broken the easel in two.' And again he laughed at himself. 'Now I am more philosophic. I do not see such terrible risks. It is like the insurance companies who ask less money for an old rider than a young one. Now I say to myself – Go slow. Perhaps it is the day, the weather, the mood. Tomorrow may be not the same.'

Later Diana came in.

'A pea-souper,' she said, and took off her coat and her bootees and went into the little bedroom to brush her hair.

'How I'd love a whisky!' she said, stalking back. There was none, so I went out and got half a bottle and we sat round the stove drinking it.

'To the summer!' said Janos.

'To Rome!' said Diana, made a little reckless by the two glasses she had already drunk.

'To Budapest!' I said.

At this Janos just perceptibly shook his head at me. At the time I thought he was warning me to be tactful because of Diana. Now I wonder.

For the rest of the evening the three of us sat round the stove. We ate spaghetti and we finished the bottle of whisky. In an unexpected way it was a pleasant evening. Each of us talked, grateful on such an evening for the stove, into which we chucked our cigarettes, for the drink and for one another. By ten one could barely see across the studio for fog. I left, but all transport had stopped, and so I came back and slept on a mattress in front of the fire. The first thing I saw in the morning were two feet over by the etching press. Janos was already working. The light was clear with only a touch of milky mist in it, the elder-bush outside the window had frost on it, and the colours on the portrait canvas looked clean and encouragingly deliberate.

DECEMBER 4

I look at the portrait, perhaps now finished. It represents a modern man thinking. It is not unlike J. But it makes him stand for something. Which is what I wanted. Just as the donor of an altar-piece was painted kneeling at the foot of the cross, I want the sitter to be involved in some drama of our time; not explicitly but implicitly in the very means and vision of the painting itself. The sketch is a better portrait if you want a portrait to cherish, to put in your locket. A woman in love with J. would prefer it every time. But I have the feeling that in painting, a too intense interest in psychology is often a form of naturalism.

This portrait now hangs in the room in which I am writing. For myself, it is in moments of doubt and despair a source of great encouragement precisely for the reasons that Janos has given. Few other people like it, however.

DECEMBER 12

The other day a mother came to see me at the school. A magnificent large Jewish woman – with her eaglet of a son – aged seventeen. Should he take up art? she asked, after I'd seen a portfolio of his work, and her eyes were fixed on me as though I were weighing a precious purchase on a pair of scales for her. 'His father was very interested in the theatre,' she added. And what was I to say? I looked at this widow prepared to fight the world for her son. I looked into the son's black, passionate, darting eyes. I looked back into the folio – the work was talented. No more as yet, no less. If, fifty years ago, a mother had come to ask you: Should my son try to fly the Atlantic? What could you have said to her? You could say something to him: something hard and disillusioning *and* inspiring. But to her? She who was likely to suffer more from the disaster.

'He must decide,' I said. And she looked at me, seeing me as a coward.

'He is only seventeen,' she said.

'He must decide,' I said again.

And she turned on me and asked: 'What do they pay you for?'

In fact, I increasingly suspect that they will not pay me for much longer. The rumours about staff cuts increase.

DECEMBER 20

I think up paintings as I might think up gifts for Christmas. But only a few of them are obtainable. Fiddled about all day. We, too, have to fight for our right to work – fight against our doubts.

1954

JANUARY 3

The painter is not important in the Western world? How wrong you are. I have just read that in Madrid after the war the body of the Duchess of Alba was exhumed in order to measure her skeleton and so establish once and for all whether it was she who lay naked for Goya in *The Maja Undressed*. The evidence was inconclusive. The curiosity is only matched by the misunderstanding. And the curiosity is endless, insatiable! Every holiday that Picasso has taken during his life has now been plotted on a map, and is printed in his catalogues along with a chart of whom he was making love to at any given time. Perhaps this will at least avoid later exhumations. Yet, Christ, it is all superstition – as primitive in its way as any magic! As bourgeois society increasingly destroys and corrupts the general, popular creative spirit, the experience of imaginative creation becomes rarer and rarer till in the end people think there is some magical secret for creativity. And so the search for this secret in the artist's private life begins: a search which is doomed to failure, for in fact 'the secret' is a massive platitude as incomprehensible to the inquisitive as their own barrenness. We create out of faith. Gerhard Marks – a noble man although his way was not mine – once said: 'It is not the function of art to relieve those without faith from their boredom.' We create to improve the world, 'to establish,' as Tolstoy wrote, 'brotherly union among men.' This is even true of Goya, agonized as he was. For him his faith was on the far side of his vision; it could not be expressed directly – it could only be served by telling the bitter truth. There is no other 'secret' but this. Certainly there isn't one in any duchess's pelvis, or for that matter in any painter's skull. Faith is of the flesh.

JANUARY 7

Laszlo inspired faith – even in the Berlin terror of 1933. Juli would never have recognized the youth she had seduced on the banks of the Tisza in that man. Laszlo developed – or perhaps just changed – far more dramatically than I did. He became very sober. Speculation was no longer free. It was tied to certain key problems with which it was his duty to concern himself. He was still young. His long face was not dried yet, and his large lips were very red. But in his eyes and in his whole poise there was a veteran's determination. He was forbidding because he was so obviously hard on himself. He was tireless, or, rather, he gave the impression of being so accustomed to being tired that the term was meaningless. When he walked away from you his jacket hung from his shoulders and his trousers from his hips as though they were never taken off, like clothes hanging for months in the Jewish second-hand shops that were being smashed up. By then he wore spectacles. He belonged to that unique international fraternity of scholars – the activist scholars of Marxism. In every photograph from 1910 onwards you find their faces. I know that beside them I look like a nineteenth-century romantic. They are short-sighted from reading and they are often frail in physique. But they have known they can change the world.

I used to see him whenever he came through Berlin. I suppose we lived in worlds almost as different from one another then as we did later. We faced a common enemy, and we were sure that when at last we arrived we should arrive together. But our trades were different, one might say. Only our occupations were not trades and they demanded from both of us more than most trades do of a man. Hence our different lives. Laszlo was a professional revolutionary. When you saw him you thought to yourself: somewhere behind this man with an historical mission there must be a man like any other – impatient, careless, at a loss. But there was not a man like any other behind him. His breaking point would not have occurred anywhere this side of the line beyond which we can all be reduced to children.

Not long after I first met him, I remember Janos talking at length about such a man, although he didn't mention his name and was more concerned, I think, with destroying any illusions I might have than with reminiscing. He told me that it was not easy for me to imagine what it meant to be a modern revolutionary. A great deal depends, he said, upon the kind of situation you find yourself in. It is one thing to be a partisan in the hills, and it is altogether another to be earning your living in an enemy city, with regular trams running and the bread baked well every night and the post punctual in the morning, where no state of war, revolution or counter-revolution is ever openly recognized. The barricades are one thing, and the police-station across the road from crowds queueing to go into the opera is another. There is a state of public emergency and martial law, and there is another state of private, apparently paranoic, but desperate vigilance.

Listen, he said. You sit by the window in an express train. It is almost night. You light a cigarette and think, relaxed, about your new destination. You lean forward to look intently at the moonlit landscape as the train slows down. A moon. A cloud that looks like a young foal. And suddenly, reflected on the window, obliterating the landscape and near, almost on top of you, you see a uniformed figure staring at you through the doorway from the corridor. You do not start or move. You wait.

You join a queue outside a butcher's shop to buy some meat. As you stand there, you notice that the front of the shop has heavy iron bars down it. And you remember K. who disappeared two years ago. He was found several months later in the middle of the night. He was sober and he was standing on the pavement in front of a butcher's shop gripping the iron bars like these with both hands, staring at the carcasses of meat, and shouting, 'For the love of God and the Holy Ghost, let me out! Let me out!' And you wait.

You go by a devious route to a specially called meeting, the papers in your pocket, folded up and put for safety between the pages of a brochure of the city's largest furnishing store. The others are there. You hear that it is necessary to alter the method for contacting. The talk is brief, for these meetings are like dives under the water, and each must surface again separately and as soon as possible. Yet, separated and framed within your brief meetings with them these seven people become more powerfully typical than can any characters separated and framed within a work of art. F., in his massive bear-like coat, with every line of his expressions, however efficient and clipped his orders, demonstrating that he is a poet. M., who should still be painted as a Venus, but who, with her husband murdered, will now only use her sex to protect an avenger, twenty-eight years old. J., squat, grinning, tricky, a mechanic, who believes that one day he will spend all his time fishing. W., ascetic lawyer and born organizer, perhaps the only one who in some corner of his heart enjoys the intrigue, because it allows him to use his surplus energy organizing the ironies of the contrast between his two lives: his public one and his underground one. H., thirty years old, an international organizer who since his youth has never stayed in one country for more than two years, but has always lived in exactly the same type of room, one-third of it taken up by a narrow bed. L., a compositor with an old-fashioned moustache, a natural anti-quarian who thinks only of the future. A., the only romantic, nicknamed the Flyer. As you think of these comrades, whose essential selves are so much simpler than the circumstances they and you are in, you imagine yourself meeting F. as a poet, M. as a beautiful woman, J. on the river bank with his rod, W. as an after-dinner raconteur, H. on some research expedition, L. showing you round his library, and A. as a popular hero. And again you wait.

He wrote no poetry then: all words had to be coded. He must have begun writing again in the Soviet Union. I left half my life's work in Berlin. How many manuscripts, music-sheets, canvases, unanswered letters, wedding invitations, unpaid bills, were left in that city that year? All to be cancelled out. If the Pompeians still lived they would look back at Pompeii as we look back at Berlin. Only we fled from men.

Laszlo remained calm and experienced. Later I heard that he was periodically in Berlin up to 1935. He was not a simple man. Ernst Thälmann presented himself to the police to protest the Party's innocence in the Reichstag fire. He never returned home. The man, whom five million people had voted for, was arrested on the spot. Laszlo understood the level of events. He could be barefaced – he went to a police station himself, where he was thought to be a Hungarian business man, to protest because his bungalow had been raided, but he was never naïve as most of us were. He understood what so few did or do – the power of the state. Indeed, perhaps we were told to go because we were known to be too innocent – we supporters of Béla Kun. 'I shan't see you' were the last words Laszlo said to me. He was beside me in the station urinal. He had come to see me off. We pissed against the same wall. That was our farewell. What I thought he meant was that he wouldn't notice me on the platform outside. He did mean that. But did he mean more? Was he six moves ahead then, too?

JANUARY 10
'Once the artist has chosen a subject it ceases to belong to Nature' – Goethe.

JANUARY 11
Going to Cornelissens to restock as much as I can afford, I dropped into the British Museum to look at the prints. The Montegna engravings. There *are* people who know what we are at, even though most of them are probably other painters. What we are at has very little to do with what is afterwards called art, and is of no great importance to the world. It doesn't matter that few understand it; it is the result and not the process that matters. When a man stands in front of a painting and realizes that up to now he has forgotten something – that is what is important. Everything else is better called technique. What we are at is only our personal problem, which is why a painting that is nothing more than a biography describing how it has been painted is valueless.

Yet there are others who understand what we face. Certain. Most intellectuals in Europe today wish for strength from their belief that human nature is infinitely varied. It is a vain wish. I gain strength from my knowledge that in any given circumstances most men are the same; it is only the circumstances that are so various. There are other men who want to paint as I do, and in front of our pages or easels, our experiences are common to each of us. There are many brotherhoods without name. And if I had to give a single piece of advice to a young painter, I would remind him of this. Then it would not seem to him so important or tragic or embittering that most of those who talk about art are entirely ignorant.

The problem of drawing. How many people believe that the Renaissance was full of great draughtsmen? It wasn't. Only three or four Renaissance artists are personally equal to Degas as a draughtsman. What the Renaissance did have was a method of drawing; one man could then teach another how to draw. Today, without a method because without tradition, one man can only tell another: Look at Nature. Look, look, and make again on paper what you can of it. Nor can we decide to invent a method. Occasionally, a method springs from a vision that can be shared. Cubism. For a short while Cubism made many fine drawings possible: drawings drawn by men who otherwise would have been indifferent draughtsmen – as many of them became again later after Cubism had revealed all that it could and had degenerated into mannerism. No, there will be no consistent method of drawing this side of Socialism. A method of drawing is the result of an identity of interest in reality. Bourgeois culture now only has a diversity of interest in fantasy. Finally, Socialism will enter even the smallest sketch-book.

JANUARY 17

Terrible quarrel with Diana. Both of us hatefully seeing – as one always realizes afterwards but not at the time – that there can never, never, never be an arbiter. Began a large etching from the Covent Garden stuff. Just a head, fruit basket, arms and hands.

Janos and Diana quarrelled in the same way, I suppose, as anyone else. Of the two, Janos was the more violent and so the first to become helpless. Diana was colder. I remember one of their quarrels at about this time. The students of a central London art school, at which I occasionally lectured, had asked Janos to go and criticize their work. His talk went down well, and afterwards a group of students surrounded him to ask questions and argue. Obviously he was enjoying himself. Amongst other things because – whatever he wrote in his journal – Janos immensely enjoyed the company of young girls for whom he was often, as he says, a romantic figure. He would eye them with open admiration, make them sit next to him, call them 'my dear' and talk endlessly. Consequently we arrived back in Fulham at least an hour later than we had expected.

It was clear as soon as we arrived that Diana was put out. They had planned to go to the cinema that evening, and now they would have to hurry.

'What kept you?' she demanded.

'It was my fault,' I put in.

'He never has any sense of time when other people are concerned.' She was dressed up for the evening, and held her head very haughtily. She looked towards Janos, but continued to speak to me. 'When it's his work, every minute's important, of course.'

'Rosie, don't be boring,' he said in a tired way.

She kept her body absolutely still and just turned her head. 'Boring! For Christ's sake! What do you think I've been for the last hour?'

'We'll take a taxi.' Janos made to go towards the door.

'That's it! Throw eight shillings away.'

'Then do not let us take a taxi.'

'I'm not going in in the middle.'

'Then let us take a taxi.'

She flung her handbag on to the table.

'There's no need to be funny. Go by yourself or with John here. I'm not coming.'

Janos went up to her to take her arm. The gentleness of his gesture was in marked contrast to the set line of his jaw.

'You'd better go straightaway,' she said very quietly. For some reason this was the last straw for Janos. He suddenly became as violent as his expression. There was a piece of drapery hanging like a curtain from the balcony that protruded over the floor near the door. He tore at it – absurdly, like a child who has had a sheet thrown over him, ripped it from the drawing-pins that fastened it to the wood, and, clumsily, all in a bundle, threw it at Diana, shouting, 'Too much! The End! Too much!' and charged out, slamming the door. Diana turned her back on me and walked over to the window.

'I'm sorry, John. So sorry,' she said very clearly.

A magnificent winter's day. A man against a sunlit window, the sky a drained blue and the man's white shirt viridian among the mahogany shadows. But that is not a painting I would any longer paint. Interiors – tents, peasant inns, old libraries, small twelve-people chapels, ships' cabins – these are one context for living, one form of habitation. Another is the crow's-nest, the observatory, the modern building open on every side. Each mode of living has its own type of painting. And I have chosen the second.

An aeroplane smoke-writing in the sky. It climbs steeply but perfectly straight – as straight as a plumb-line falls. Then it levels out, and starts turning to the left in a slow curve, like that of the deltoid. To pilot a quill through the sky! We have our victories. And as the wind nibbles at the white line, it becomes serrated and soft on the edge that the wind is nibbling, as the edge of a torn piece of linen, until in the end it is erased. But any one who has seen it has had the chance of pondering on how large man can write. He can brand the sky with its noun. Such is my arrogance as a painter. Such is our type of painting.

JANUARY 28

Our ballast is death; it is this that gives us our speed.

FEBRUARY 6

Have worked this last week on a small canvas of a couple on a beach.

My classes at the school are going to be reduced to one afternoon and evening a week. A loss of £8.

A specific hardship brings out the best in Diana – perhaps because it is something concrete to fight. When I told her, she said, 'Don't worry, Jimmy; we'll manage.'

It was when I heard this news that I decided to make a concentrated effort to get Janos an exhibition.

I asked him for a portfolio of drawings and water-colours and also some photographs. He gave them to me, neither with nor without enthusiasm. All that he recognized was the trouble I was taking. 'You should get on with your own work,' he once said, 'but thank you.'

Diana was delighted with my plan; at least partly because she loved the intrigue. They were feeble strings we were pulling, but we were pulling them, and that meant for her that life was set moving for once. She was always taking me aside when I arrived at the studio and asking me what galleries I had tried, and what had they said, and would so-and-so, whom she'd known, be of any help because he had once bought several Sickerts from such-and-such a dealer. She was like a mother plotting a Christmas present, and she ransacked her memory for ideas and suggestions. Yet because she hadn't an inkling about either the value or the comparative character of Janos's work, she never understood what the real difficulties were.

I went to all the leading West End galleries. Although every gallery sells paintings by, say, Renoir and Boudin, they vary in character a great deal. Some are like very old-established shops for gentlemen, and in these the reaction to the unknown painter hawking his work round is frankly professional: 'I like the work, but I'm afraid we just couldn't sell it. I'd be prepared to put a couple of your things into a mixed show, if you like.' Others are like car show-rooms. And in these a man behind the desk reading the Financial Times looks up and says, 'Definitely. We have our regular artists and frankly we're booked up until 1960.' Others are informal, like Bohemian drinking clubs, and a girl at a typewriter, who is probably a wife or mistress, says, 'Leave them here, and I'll try to get Ronnie to look at them when he comes in.' Yet others are like hotel reception lounges with people constantly coming and going and a book of bookings. 'If we get a cancellation, we just might be able to do something for you.'

With the slight advantage my job gave me, I was able to approach individuals in each of the galleries, and so was able, to some extent, to get beyond this stock system of stalling.

I do not propose to tell the full story of all the negotiations with each of the dozen galleries I approached. The variations from one to another were roughly according to the same pattern of treatment as I have just described. My adventure with the Garden Gallery was in no way unusual, and it can stand in for them all. The Garden is one of the smartest and most 'adventurous' of the London galleries; it is a cross between the Bohemian club and the car salesroom. One of its directors is the writer on aesthetics – Robert De Quincey.

Seeing him at a cocktail party, I decided that this was an opportune moment for approaching him. He was talking to a man whom Janos had once christened Marcus Aurelius: an immensely fat man and a well-known critic, whose Christian name is, in fact, Marcus. De Quincey is thin, like a youth – although he must be at least forty.

'Supposing I bring in a customer,' Marcus Aurelius was saying, 'who buys a couple of thousand pounds worth, what would you do?'

'You'd have to warn us that you were going to do so. We simply must insist on that, you see, to safeguard ourselves from everybody claiming they've brought customers in.'

'Of course. I quite understand. But then?'

'Naturally, we'd give you your ten per cent.'

The word 'naturally' was pronounced as if it were a word of maximum authority; the equivalent of somebody else saying, 'I give you my word.'

'Bon! I just wanted to check up. Because one or two galleries, whose names I won't mention, are no longer honouring that tradition.'

I brought the subject round to painters and asked if they'd heard of Janos Lavin. They had not.

'We're always interested in a new name, though,' De Quincey suggested. 'How old is he?'

'Over fifty.'

'Oh. That does make it a teeny bit difficult.'

'What's his work like?' asked Marcus Aurelius.

'Difficult to describe. But I think very highly of it.'

'German?'

'No, Hungarian.'

'Over fifty and mid-European. That does make it difficult. But why not ask him to bring something round to us?'

'It would be better if you went to his studio.'

'You know what it is, we don't really like doing that unless we have something to go on. It can be so embarrassing. Ask him to bring something round.'

Ten days or so later I went round to the gallery with the portfolio. Strangely, Marcus Aurelius was also there, presumably waiting for his customer or his percentage. He walked up to me and smiled. His smile was a kind of leer, directed against both himself and the world in general.

'What about your Hungarian?'

'What about your two-thousand-pound client?'

'Three thousand now. But don't sound so bloody prim about it. I don't like the bloody system any more than you do. But it's sentimental to deny it if it exists. And, anyway, why shouldn't we sell our knowledge?'

'Is it knowledge or the power of persuasion?'

'If so, that's even rarer, my dear fellow, even rarer.'

De Quincey was not at his desk, so I went downstairs into the lower gallery. It was full of pear-drop perfume from wet nail varnish. The plump, middle-aged secretary who was using it, sat cross-legged, her skirt rucked slightly over her knees. On top of her head her greying hair was only barely touched with purple. Near her desk an Italian youth sat on a stool. He was employed by the gallery as a messenger, framer and general shifter. At this moment he appeared to be fixing some black theatrical hair on to an African mask.

'Is Mr De Quincey about yet?'

'I don't think he's come in. Raffaele – go and see!'

She addressed this last remark to the Italian with startling roughness and vehemence. The boy slowly got off his stool, looked at the woman with an expression of contemptuous pity and slouched out. As her eyes followed him, her lids flickered. After he had disappeared through the door into the back rooms, she turned round and stiffened as she remembered I was still there.

'What a morning!'

The Italian came back with De Quincey.

'Ah! Your Hungarian! You have some of his work? Let's go into the other room, I mentioned it to Ninette. She'll be in shortly.'

We went through the door into the inner room. The carpet there was golden. The curtains and the chairs – high backed for placing pictures on – were the same colour in velvet. The only picture on the walls was a greatly enlarged photograph of the head of Nijinsky. It was unframed, but a sheet of plate-glass, gilded at the edges, was fastened over it with golden clips. In the centre of the room stood a black, lacquered easel. On a side table there were several decanters and a box of cigars. Without any reason for thinking so, one had the impression that the room was sound-proof.

'Now you simply must understand,' said De Quincey, adjusting the window, 'that we're absolutely booked up for the next year. I say this now before we look at the work so that you really can't think –'

'Yes, I quite understand.'

I opened the portfolio on the table. De Quincey began turning the sheets over. He did this by taking hold of the bottom right-hand corner of each one between his finger and thumb. On his middle finger was a ring. He turned the drawings over slowly but quite regularly. An innocent observer would have said he was counting them. His lips were indrawn, but his eyes observed blankly, passively – as though he were looking, like a checker, for one particular thing, a particular fault which he had not yet come across. He came to the last drawing, looked up and inhaled from his cigarette.

'Interesting.'

'You like them?'

'He clearly has talent. But it's work, don't you know, that very much belongs to the twenties and thirties.'

'Do you think that matters?'

'Not necessarily.' He went over to make another adjustment to the window. 'This central heating is positively breath-taking. No. What I feel, you see, is that somebody like your friend belongs to a generation – how old is he, by the way? – the generation of what I call Desperate Optimism.' He was now leaning against the window-frame, rubbing the back of one hand against the velvet curtain. 'It's the same with Léger and Corb. and Mondriaan. All of them tried to fight Chaos with Order. And you just can't do it. The reality of our time is chaotic whether we like it or not. And anything that rejects that reality becomes mechanical. Look at Klee. He was a man who accepted this chaotic, irrational reality, and the result was he produced poetry. Take Picasso. He's the one man of his generation who's still contemporary. Why? Because fundamentally he's destructive. But the Desperate Optimists, as I call them – they're sentimentalists at heart. They idealize the machine and what's called The People. But, believe me, people just aren't like that. No one wants to live in a Corbusier. And why should they? Take the films and the weeklies – that's where you'll find the clue to the *popular imagination – and it's not so far from Dostoyevsky and Kafka as you might suppose. But people like your friend here, with his calm, sterilized Hope and Beauty – they're as out of touch as the Pre-Raphaelites really. Of course it's talented work – very. But in the end it's boring.'*

He smiled and opened his hands with a shrug of the shoulders, like a conjurer who, whilst talking, has made a rabbit disappear.

The door opened. And a woman with cropped red hair, wearing a well-cut pale green coat and skirt, marched into the room. She threw her large black handbag on to one of the chairs. Round one of her wrists was a massive silver bracelet, in the form of two dogs running after each other. Her sunburnt arms made the darkish silver look as if it were lead.

'Christ!' she announced. 'What a morning. It's the Lord Mayor's Show or something, and it took me twenty minutes, twenty I promise you, to find a taxi!'

De Quincey said, 'Here are the drawings I told you about, darling.'

'Good. I'll be back after a scratch.'

And she marched out again. When she came back, De Quincey sprang to attentive activity. He no longer philosophized but served. He opened the portfolio again at the first drawing, took it out, went over to one of the golden chairs, stood behind it and leant the drawing on the seat against the back of it. He first looked down at the draw-ing from above – seeing it of course upside down – and then towards Ninette. His eyebrows were slightly raised – ready to follow through into a full expression of either admiration or amusement. He made a test.

'Intéressant. Non?'

Ninette put one hand on her hips and continued to look at the drawing with an expression which I have only otherwise seen on the faces of some of the most successful and intelligent farmers at a cattle market; what might be called a meat expression. She then abruptly turned away and went over to the table where she seized all the drawings in her fist, and sat down with them on her lap in an armchair.

'Bobbie, my glasses?'

De Quincey gave her the massive black handbag.

'Thanks, darling.'

She took out a pair of heavy, red-framed spectacles and put them on. After she had looked at each work, she put it on the floor beside her. Occasionally, before putting it down, she would hold it out at arm's length in front of her and lean back in the chair, her legs apart, to study it from a distance. De Quincey stood behind her. Once he leant forward and moved his forefinger over the paper. He said nothing, however. And having made the gesture, he straightened himself up and felt the side of his hair. Ninette put the last drawing on the floor, leant back, took off her glasses and dangled them from her hand.

'I think they've got something. Whether we could do anything for him is another matter. They're a bit unimaginative – but they've got simplicity. How long's he been here?'

'Since before the war.'

'Strange. Because I was going to say that there's a strong peasant feeling here.' She shoved her thumb down towards the sheaf on the floor.

De Quincey walked over to his previous position by the window from which he had explained what he meant by Desperate Optimism.

'They've got simplicity. Certainly,' he said. 'But I'm not, don't you know, surprised. Somehow I've seen it before.'

Ninette completely ignored the remark and stretched out her dog-braceleted arm and picked up a drawing from the floor. 'This drawing of a figure. What is it? Never mind. The point is it's innocent. It's out of this world. It's innocent. On the other side of puberty, Bobbie.' She prodded the paper with her finger, and looked up.

'Is he a very simple man?'

'Terribly,' I said.

She screwed up her eyes at me. The telephone rang. De Quincey edged his way out through a crowd that wasn't there.

Ninette went over to the telephone.

'Mimi. Angel. Do come round. . . .'

Mimi began to tell some long story. Ninette sat on the edge of the table and fiddled with the back of her knee.

'No, don't worry. We'll do something else. But come round, angel, because I've got some unusual drawings to show you by an old Hungarian.'

The secretary came in and said in a tired voice:

'A Mr Cecil R. Hooper is asking for you.'

'I'll be up in a moment. Get Raffaele to bring the new Krupper down here.'

'You mean the large black one?'

'No, the smaller one that's just been framed. Moon No. 2.'

I began collecting the folio together.

'Could you leave them here till tomorrow?'

'If you're interested – yes.'

'I'd like to show them to one or two people.'

Raffaele brought in a canvas. Ninette glanced at it.

'Not that one! I told you. The small one. The one with red in it. And spots, not streams!' She sighed in exasperation. We said good-bye.

In the outer gallery Marcus Aurelius was still prowling about.

'Any luck?'

'Can't say.'

'Come and have some coffee.'

'I'm afraid I must go now.'

'Then look,' he stared hard at me, his head leaning forward towards me, but his hands in his trousers pockets pulling him back on his heels. 'Could you lend me a pound till tomorrow?'

'I'm afraid I haven't got that much.'

'Never mind,' he said, doubly smiling. 'Doesn't matter at all. I'll get it off De Quincey.'

It was several days before I went back. Ninette was in the main gallery. The girl who was sitting on her table I took to be Mimi since she was wearing an identical dog-bracelet.

'Have you been able to decide anything?' I asked Ninette. For a moment she looked blank. 'Janos Lavin,' I reminded her. She took off her red glasses and smiled up at me.

'I'm afraid it's No. Why don't you try Tommy?'

'Is this the Hungarian?' interrupted Mimi.

Ninette nodded and momentarily looked down at the papers on the table.

'Thank you,' I said.

Not until half an hour later did I remember that I had forgotten the folio. I went back. The two women had gone and De Quincey was telling a client about the painter of their present exhibition.

'. . . and in Paris he was absolutely penniless.'
His lids came down over his eyes at the thought. Then he saw me.
'Excuse me,' I said, 'I've come for the folio.'
De Quincey disengaged himself, took my arm, and led me to the
stairs, whispering in my ear, like a barrister confiding to a colleague
outside the court-room.
'I'm afraid we can't do anything at the moment.'
And he gave me the folio of the unproven case.
In this way I failed to get Janos his exhibition.

FEBRUARY 8

There are those who proudly dig up with a spade the root vegetables they have sown and tended and cared for. There are
others who in wild grass as high as their breasts pick the hap-
hazard berries. In one of these two ways most pursue their
desires. We must be as patient as the first type and as improvi-
dent as the second.

FEBRUARY 23

Working on small things, I think more and more of *The Games*
canvas.

FEBRUARY 27

George Trent came round. He liked the work. He said he was
soon to have an exhibition. George will not compromise, but he
expects recognition, acclaim. From this expectation a turning
point comes in our lives. For one half of a life you work, spurred
on by this expectation. During the second half you work to prove
to yourself that you can do without it, that the loss of the illusion
has made no difference. Then gradually you forget altogether.
You work in order to be able to die painting.

I remember going to see an old painter in Berlin, a friend of
Corinth's. After lunch he said to me, 'I think I'll go upstairs
now because I'm tired – and do a little painting.' How comic
that seemed to me then. But not so much now.

MARCH 1

What we mean by Socialism can be clearly defined in economic
terms. But the effects, the changes in man that Socialist econo-

mic relations can bring about, are so numerous that each can make his own list.

I live, work, for a state where the more honest the son the less the mother need fear; where every worker has a sense of responsibility, not because he is appealed to but because he has responsibility; where the only *élite* are the old; where every tragedy is admitted as such; where women are not employed to use their sex to sell commodities – finally this is a much greater degradation than prostitution; where the word freedom has become unnecessary because every ability is wanted; where prejudice has been so overcome that every man is able to judge another by his eyes; where every artist is primarily a craftsman; where every Imperialist leader has been tried by his former victims and, if found guilty, been shot by a contingent of his own General Staff whose lives have been spared for this purpose.

MARCH 4

Diana's father has sent her £40 as a birthday present. I bought her a dispatch-case. We had a party. J. and the Hancocks and Leonard Gough came round, and we drank wine. Len said he had done the painting of his wife and I must go and see it.

The Games must be as large as I can paint it.

MARCH 10

I cannot sleep. I look round the studio, at my life's work.

It is not possible for me to imagine myself in Budapest, for to be there would be to be rid of all that agony of conscience that has now become part of my daily life: to be there would be to be certain. But I can imagine a painter in Budapest. He may be painting pictures to defend the steel plants. Or he may be working on his own, submitting only a small part of his work for official viewing. But whichever way it is, he belongs to – it is not anything as generalized as 'a socialist society'; yet it is something wider and more diverse than the Party. He is working in a wind. Here it is utterly still. I have quiet in which to work. Certainly. Certainly. If I fight for it. If I fight against all that comes from being unwanted. Nor do I say that like a waif. Looking round, I have no wish to produce what *is* wanted. The painter in Budapest has a very different battle. In one way or another he is fighting for his place among his fellow-men; he is fighting about the terms on which his contribution is not just wanted but demanded. I have no choice but to paint as I must. But I would like to be a useful man again.

The difference between Laszlo and me was perhaps the constant difference between the revolutionary activist and the revolutionary artist. I always took victory for granted. He could never afford to. Maybe events have proved him right, but in the most unexpected way. He is dead because the victory was threatened, and I am left with only my obstinate prophetic vision.

Here I write down whatever comes into my head or floods through my heart. But on the canvas it is never so direct – and cannot be so. The realities I see and understand are on my side of a curtain. I study them and commit myself to them. Yet my hands work on the other side, trying to re-discover what I see on my side, but always limited by the medium which is the only reality *they* have to work with. Many comrades want that curtain ripped down, and when I look round and see all the dishonest purposes for which it is used today – all the confidence tricks that it can cover, I sympathize. But you can't. Rip the curtain down and consider art in the same light as you consider life, and you will create only trivialities. It is so simple. Put a bronze replica next to flesh, and who will look twice at the bronze?

The groans of lovers as they make love are more real than the greatest lyric poetry ever written. But they cannot be preserved. Art is not a means of pickling. And as soon as you admit that, you have hung up the curtain again. Yet it is not really like a curtain. What separates my hands when working from my direct experience of my subject is not a barrier in space like a curtain. It is more like a barrier in time. Between the idea I have and the work I produce, there is the same difference as between my action yesterday and its final consequence tomorrow. Intentions, good or bad, are no more important in art than in life. Any action is judged by its consequences, and those consequences are conditioned by factors so beyond the scope of our intentions that we recognize them as Necessity. In art there is also necessity. Finally the necessities of art correspond to those of life. There is no magic. But the finality of the correspondence is a long way off and beyond present understanding. I know Poussin answers a human need; but I can only see how he answered the needs of art. Between the idea I have and the work I produce come the necessities of art. Again I do not know exactly what these necessities are. I can only guess at them by foreseeing the consequences of lines, colours, forms within what will eventually become – to an extent that I cannot imagine whilst working – an unchangeable picture. When an artist works, he straddles time.

MARCH 14

Every possibility is now coming into *The Games*. Large. What I wrote the other night was demonstrated this afternoon when we went to see Len's painting of his wife. There is no curtain for Len. Yet how coldly my theories strike me when outside the studio. Len is happy. Why talk of art? And who would choose even Poussin as against living shoulders beneath warm, golden hair?

It was a Sunday, and we went round to the flat above the butcher's shop late in the afternoon. Mrs Hancock had just had a bath and was still wearing a housecoat, with her hair tumbling down her back.

'You look like a figurehead,' said Janos gallantly.

'Don't be silly,' she laughed, her hands overlapping the top of her coat.

Soon she went to the window and shouted, 'Come up, Len! Mr Lavin's here.'

Len opened the door of the shed at the back of the shop where he painted, waved, peered short-sightedly up at the window, and lolloped across the yard on his ostrich legs. He always painted with his beret on – it was a symbol, perhaps of Sunday Vie de Bohème. When he appeared in the doorway of the living-room, a streak of paint on his face, and his large red hands with little rubbed marks of white and blue on them, he looked down at us all and said:

'Ah! the perfume of turps! You can keep your roses. How are you now?'

We sat down and had tea. Then Janos asked:

'What about the painting?'

'*Which one?*'

'*Of your wife.*'

'*Blow me. Of course you haven't seen it.*'

'*I'm sure they aren't really interested,*' said Mrs Hancock emphatically.

'*I'm sure they are,*' replied Len, already at the door. '*You mustn't be modest about it, Vee. After all, it's only a painting.*'

After he had gone, Mrs Hancock busied herself collecting the tea-things together. The gas-fire scorched away in the room full of new highly polished furniture. Then she looked up and said:

'*I wish I'd never posed for the thing.*'

'*Don't you like it, then?*'

'*It's not that. It's all so silly. All this fuss about it. Len went on and on about it till I agreed. And now he shows it to everybody – like a ten-pound note. He doesn't consider my feelings at all.*'

'*You should be flattered, Mrs Hancock,*' said Janos.

'*I was, and it's a very flattering picture. But no one wants compliments like that paid in public. It's a private thing, to my way of thinking – all that sort of thing.*'

Len came back with the painting. It was small, only about a foot high, and on oiled paper which had afterwards been varnished. Mrs Hancock took the tea-tray out into the kitchen. Len handed the picture to Janos in his huge hand – the nail of his thumb square-shaped like the base of a shovel.

'*The Venus of Fulham,*' he said loudly, and then went over to the kitchen door and put his arm round his wife's shoulder.

The painting was roughly like a poster for the Folies Bergère. There was nothing amateurish about Len's paintings. Technically they were painstakingly skilful. Once Janos had asked him, '*Why do you not use a bigger brush? You tickle the canvas like a Chinese torturer!*'

Len had looked at the painting in question through his metal-rimmed spectacles as though Janos had complained that a fly had got mixed up with the paint. But he had not understood.

In this picture, Mrs Hancock, sitting on an upholstered stool, was wearing her housecoat, which was open at the top to disclose one shoulder and her breasts. Farther down, the coat crossed her lap and fell behind her bare legs. On her feet she wore high-heeled shoes. The housecoat was golden, her hair the colour of marigolds, and her flesh like pink satin. *Behind the figure was a mirror on the wall, and in this was reflected a tiny self-portrait of Len himself, wearing his beret. Although entirely innocently so, it was one of the most immodest pictures I have ever seen. It had all the stream-lined provocation of brassière advertisements; and at the same time it had a particularity which these never have. The eyes and nipples stared out at one with bridal clarity. Janos leant the picture against the armchair opposite and gazed at it intently.*

'*I know it's a bit patchy,*' *said Len.*

'*It is very remarkable,*' *Janos announced.* '*I could not have done it myself like that.*'

'*Come off it,*' *said Len with complete sincerity.* '*You're too modest. You could have done it standing on your head if you'd wanted to!*'

MARCH 17

I read today of the suicide of de Staël. He was a better painter than he knew. Any suicide is the result of a lack of recognition. The man believes there is no sense in this world because there is no comprehension. If he happens to be an artist, the missing recognition will be, at least partly, connected with the attitude of other people to his work. De Staël had been successful and was acclaimed. Ponder on this. Capitalist society is incapable of rewarding the artist, incapable of granting true success. The social salute has the same ring to it as the last shot of Vincent's revolver. 'Even the highest intellectual productions are only recognized and accepted by the bourgeois because they are presented as direct producers of material wealth and wrongly shown to be such.' I marked that passage long ago.

Cubism is to us what Anatomy was to Michelangelo. The energy of my athletes is in their juxtaposition and colours. Never in their muscles.

MARCH 20

I need money to begin *The Games.* I cannot paint it on board: I need canvas.

The athlete is one of the few individuals under capitalism who demonstrates purely and hopefully the process of civilization. Capitalism has brought with it a higher and wider degree of self-consciousness than ever existed before. This self-consciousness is an advance beyond a life of intuition. But the final creative aim of self-consciousness must be to consciously lose itself, to return to a reliance upon intuition *within certain consciously created limits*. To live as the athlete runs or jumps or swims.

The bloody competitiveness of capitalism has prevented this ever happening. Having achieved self-consciousness, it needs firm confidence to lose it again deliberately. Capitalism has been incapable of producing such a climate of confidence.

The same thing affects art. Capitalism has finally destroyed the traditions of art it once inherited or created, because art also needs the same kind of controlled liberation of intuition – in both artist and spectator.

It is because there can be no controlled freedom of intuition that there is so much pure irrationalism in art today – the cries of help to the subconscious, and the return to savage, unlimited, pointless 'intuition'.

But the athlete demonstrates the point best. In pure athletics it is the individual's intuition that is liberated. In sport the liberation is collective. I have seen games of football in which I have glimpsed all I believe the productive relations among men might be.

APRIL 10

This time it is Léger's *Les Constructeurs*, but it is often happening like this. You see a work you like because you admire the spirit of it, and you say to yourself, yes, that is a fine invention. Then later, perhaps even years later, you find yourself watching a person, a scene, an object, which might have been the origin of the painting you admired, and suddenly you realize that it wasn't invention at all but truth that the work was based on. And this realization is always, for me anyway, very moving. Because it emphasizes all the originality, courage, effort that lay behind the presenting of that truth which looked like an invention. It is like listening to a story-teller because he tells good stories and then suddenly realizing that he is talking about his own life, about himself in the third person. I am still preparing for *The Games*.

I brought two students back to the studio today. Both young fellows from Leeds. They admired the studio because it was larger and lighter than their own bed-sitting-rooms.

I showed them about twenty canvases. God knows whether they liked them or whether they were just impressed by their skill. It's a strange business, this showing of your work to friends. You stand back and look at the easel with them. And there on it is this thing you've once shared everything with. Sometimes it is like going to identify the face of a dead friend in a morgue. Sometimes it is like peering through a window to watch your young daughter playing unawares in the sunlight. Yet this part of your feeling is unimportant. This is the price you've paid. The value of the picture is another thing altogether. That you must read in the faces of your visitors – and in the verdict of your own reason, if you can hear it through the din of your protesting obstinacy. The question of what we should do without this obstinacy is academic. If it is preserved until you are thirty-five or so, you can never lose it. You'll twist, destroy, duck under any fact which really dangerously threatens it. You'll fight to stay in your state of obstinacy like a fish fights to stay in water.

Diana came in just before they left. She made coffee for us, and asked them about their homes – of which I knew nothing. Diana, on occasions like this, always makes me realize that I function on a very narrow front. She instinctively wants everything in play, so that no connexion, no lever, need pass unused or unnoticed. I admire this in her, for it is another kind of obstinacy. She would like to perform with V.I.P.s, but she persists even with students.

APRIL 25

The plan for *The Games* becomes more definite. The final canvas must be as big as the studio will hold. Unless the figures are at least life-size, their simplification will seem too schematic. This is one of the lessons of the Douanier Rousseau. His greatest pictures would have seemed merely quaint if they had been book-size. The problem of scale is not very clearly understood today. Many paintings painted are too big, inflated. If you want to paint a personal possession – and we can possess a cornfield, an apple, the face of a friend, a city skyline – then you must not over-enlarge it, for it will become vulgar, like all possessions that are made to appear more imposing than they are. But if you want to paint a legend that expresses a way of life that you cannot possess but only contribute to, then you must paint it large so that it remains impersonal, unpossessable. Historically this problem has mostly looked after itself. Whenever a society has been consciously concerned with its collective legends, painters have been given large walls or ceilings to paint them on. When private property itself became the legend, the small easel picture became the new art form. Today our handicap is a simple one; we await the time when people will no longer just use walls for hiding themselves and their property.

MAY DAY

Drew all day from an Indian model. Diana clearly thinks I am mad, but she adds she knows somebody on the British Section of the Olympic Games Committee. Later, I tell her, later.

MAY 3

I want to use the minimum of foreshortening and as many frontal views as possible. The overall image must be somewhat like that of a posed photograph: yet not static. As so often, I go back to Poussin. But the visual elegance of an age is closely related to its manners. We no longer kiss hands. We grip arms, or we embrace like Rembrandt's Jews. Thus, where Poussin hangs a garland I shall paint the athlete's number – solid black numerals on white.

MAY 4

A dark outline must never be used against the lightest tone on the canvas. If it is, it will desert its own figure or object and become the border of that lightest tone which it will bring to the utmost surface of the picture.

MAY 5

Where Poussin uses the bough of a tree, I shall use hurdles.

The faces must be open like vases. This was Michelangelo's secret as much as it is Léger's. It is the energy of their bodies that fills their faces with meaning. It is the opposite of Rembrandt. In Rembrandt it is the expression that gives the body meaning. Moreover, by expression in that sense we always mean tragic expression. Happiness is curiously impersonal. That is why we can identify ourselves so easily with a happy pair of lovers, and even share their happiness. At a bus stop today I saw an old man and an old woman. There was a short queue and the old woman was at the head of it. The old man comes up and stands behind her. Nobody else in the queue objects. But the old woman turns round and, swearing, tells him to take his proper place in the queue – at the back. He says that it is none of her business. She replies that everyone taking their turn is her business and everybody's business. And so they wrangle and swear at each other. She turns her back on him. And he stares with loathing at the grey bun on the back of her neck. Then she turns round and looks him up and down, noticing the buttons that are missing from his shabby suit, the frayed cuffs, the undone shoe-lace. You're a filthy man, she says, and her mouth turns down over the words. The bus arrives. And they get on it together and sit next to one another. They are husband and wife. Their faces, harsh and individual in their suffering, have been recorded many times in the history of painting. You will find them in Cosimo Tura, and in Michelangelo himself – when he tried to destroy the Sistine ceiling by painting the Last Judgement – in Breughel, in Rembrandt, in El Greco, in Goya, in Daumier, in Grünewald, in Picasso. Their suffering challenges your individuality, puts you on your guard, and cautiously, because you're playing with fire, you take in as much of the truth about your life as you dare. God knows I should be able to paint like that myself; I have seen enough. But another vision persists. Calm. Permanence. The stability of the anonymous. The pride of the artist searching, not directly for his soul, but for ever-increased skill. Piero, Raphael, Veronese, Poussin, David, Cézanne, Léger, Brancusi and, in his distracted, Calvinist way, Mondriaan too. The art historians make the differentiation between Romantic and Classic, but that has little sense before the nineteenth century. And anyway, Delacroix, arch-romantic, immensely admired Raphael. No, the difference is between those who believe that life is essentially tragic and those who do not. I do not. The individual is tragic. But the individual can also question this tragedy and so become heroic: heroism consists of understanding that the achievement can be greater than the individual achiever.

MAY 14

I need at least £40 to begin this painting.

MAY 16

I woke up thinking I was crazy: not dramatically so, just a little touched. Why paint a canvas 20 by 30 feet that nobody has commissioned? Am I suffering from illusions of grandeur? In the shaving-mirror I looked my usual goat's-head self. And so I went to Cornelissens and ordered the canvas on account. The pure ground colours in their bottles are like uncut diamonds – on which we must work. But unfortunately many of them cost almost as much as diamonds. I do not worry about my financial position. I have got used to it, as a man can get used to a wooden leg. But sometimes I dream of running. I dream of a sheet of glass 50 yards long and behind it, at night, the lights of a studio, sails of white canvas, a table with fifteen people round it, arguing, drinking, joking in the way that people can if they meet regularly. Diana happy as she once was, cognac, new magazines and a pupil to clean my brushes.

MAY 27

It is the afternoons that almost defeat me. However little I eat for lunch, I feel sleepy, to such an extent that for about an hour I find myself thinking, dreaming of rest as the supreme sensuous pleasure. I am going to develop the idea of the tiles which I used in *The Swimmers*. Behind the athletes there will be a flat surface on which there'll be a design, a kind of free frieze of them in action. But the drawing of these actions will be interrupted by the figures in front. The lines of the drawings behind must seem like lassoes whirling round the figures in front. And on the wall within the picture I am painting clouds. It occurs to me that I invent this wall within my picture because I have no actual one to paint on.

JUNE 18
Have worked for several weeks on many studies. None is quite right yet. The canvas has come, but remains unpaid for. I want the painting to look as fresh, as unstruggled with, as new wet paint on a front door.

JUNE 20
Desires, like foliage, are blown away.

JUNE 21
Have borrowed £20 from Max. He came, looked at the canvas, said it was like a bloody back-drop and then began to tap-dance in front of it. The incorrigible Max. 'How much does the scenery cost?' he asked. I told him, and added that I hadn't paid for it yet. Thereupon he took out his wallet, counted out twenty pounds and said, 'Borrow them.' That's all. But as he did so he looked at me with his ironic after-joke expression. This was his reproach to me for my refusal to guarantee his fare to America. One of his lessons on how to be irresponsible. I took them.

JUNE 23
Did I wrong Max when I wrote that? He is a man to whom I cannot be just. He is the opposite side of my coin.

JUNE 27
The sketches are still not right. They are too spontaneous.

JUNE 30
A good day. I become more and more convinced that the ability to work well depends upon how I sleep. I work in my sleep, and next day through the process of working I remember what I discovered the night before. A piece of work is good when I recognize its face, as a result of that earlier and up to that moment unremembered encounter.

JULY 3

Rain and grey London heat for four days now. In this canvas I want the sound of rain on a skylight to be unimaginable. But I can only achieve this by intelligence, by using all that every other painter has ever taught me. I tell my students that there are no tricks in art. (One of the students I brought round here three months ago came up to me yesterday and said how much the visit had thrilled him. Considering what I felt at the time, I must beware of becoming paranoic – it is a grave danger.) I tell my students that there are no tricks in art. Which is true enough in its way, for most tricks are copied mannerisms: copies of copies. But the skill we need and acquire so slowly – what is that if it is not, in another sense, a trick?

The only difference between the two kinds of trick is that in one case you are just trying to get the better of your picture, and that means you are playing a trick on yourself, deceiving yourself, pretending you have more feeling, more skill, more experience, than you actually have, and in the other case you are trying to get the better of your subject, of reality. Getting the better of the real – is to be an artist. How tired I am. Sometimes I wonder why I write these pages at all. Perhaps to stop myself painting bad pictures. There are so many things – too many – that are nothing to do with painting at all.

JULY 20

Began a week ago on the large canvas. It looks much smaller now.

The 20 by 30 feet canvas fantastically distorted the whole studio. It was like a partition that divided the room into two, making both halves seem unfamiliarly cramped. Standing in the doorway, you could only see the back of the canvas. On the far side you could hear the noises of a man moving about. You shouted and, if he was amenable, Janos would squeeze himself between one end of the canvas and the wall and come out to talk. If he was not amenable, he would continue working as if in another room. On the far side of the canvas, before it was painted and whilst it was still white, one had the impression – despite the skylight – of being in a white-washed cellar. After the painting had been begun, watching Janos working on it was like watching a bill-poster on his ladder. Diana joked, with some justice, that it was like living on a building site.

JULY 28
I am beginning to correct. Bits of it are too overcrowded.

AUGUST 4
How difficult it is to avoid suggestion, to turn down invitations from the paint. And how necessary. The clouds look bloody silly.

AUGUST 5
There are days – and today has been one – when I pace about the studio as useless as an apprentice whose master is away. I mix up the colours. And then I can do nothing; I look at the canvas and with the apprentice's secret and idle ambition I say to myself, one day I shall do better. Then I turn on the wireless.

AUGUST 8
London clinker-coloured on a summer evening. The runner carrying the flame through the night. What an idea that is! And visually there is something metaphorical about it: for an athlete's exertion actually attenuates his body in the same way as the flickering light-and-shade of a flare appears to attenuate it. There is a chiaroscuro of exertion. Géricault was master of it.

   I owe the National Health £20.

AUGUST 9
If we find it, there is – so far as our senses are concerned – a perfect equation in every pose, every body. I know nothing more satisfying than finding that equation. One is gratified at the same instant in two so different ways. It is then as though a Roman viaduct were the proud creation of – no more than a perfect kiss. For evidence of this look at Poussin – where dancing figures make their Colosseum. This is the only magic I allow myself.

AUGUST 10
At the moment I'm good for nothing else but this canvas. At

South Kensington I saw a West Indian woman with a magnificent head. I realize now that it was a mistake to ever think of including figures of different races. Let them be – men and women. It is essential that we realize that painting has become a very limited art. Most of all the Ministers of Culture must realize that. There is so much that painting cannot do now. This is not the result of any poverty of intention. It is the result of the abundance of the means of expression at our disposal. I believe that if Giotto were alive today he would rightly make films; so would Goya. But not Raphael, Piero, Titian, Poussin, Cézanne.

AUGUST 20

It is so hot that I am working only in a pair of trousers. Diana goes and sun-bathes at Putney. When it is hot I remember my mother. 'Not a cool place in God's oven,' she would say. And I can see with absolute clarity the St Peter I carved for her from a faggot with the broken head of an axe. She hung it above her bed under the real crucifix.

SEPTEMBER 7

There are two types of colour: apparent colour and actual colour. Apparent colours – the colour of the sky, the sea, sunlight on earth, shadow on flesh or any object in light – always imply within themselves the victory of the colour they present over all other possible colours. Somewhere in the blue-black of a night sky there is a vanquished red, a vanquished green, even a vanquished yellow. We have to create this vibrancy not separately in each colour we apply, but through the relationship one to another of the colours we use on each canvas. In terms of colour we have to transform depth into breadth.

SEPTEMBER 11

Went to the local cinema with Diana. Supposing *The Games* was projected on to that screen (which is almost exactly the same proportion as the canvas) for five minutes. No movement. No comment. Just there in its colour and its entirety. How many seconds would pass before the audience started talking and looking away?

In front of a mute canvas I sometimes think of the gift of a singer amongst people who still sing. He has a power which no other artist can have; he can make his audience participate. On one level it is commonplace enough. It is what happens in the pubs down the Fulham Road every Saturday night. On another level it is what fishermen can hear as they approach the coast, or what an old man can hear from his bed at harvest-time. But on either level it is a mysterious power, this singing, which, like smoke, is one of the humblest signs of human habitation. Most of the songs are sad – like the cry of a gull, blown inland, over a forest; yet as they are sung, the singers hear each other, and often also touch one another, and so by this method share their losses until finally what is shared is greater than the loss. Thinking this in front of the mute canvas, I sometimes sing to myself: *Szeretnék – szántani.*

This is a Hungarian children's song of which a rough translation is as follows:
I would plough
And drive with six great oxen.
And if my sweetheart would come to hold the plough
To drive with six great oxen,
I would plough with my sweetheart.

SEPTEMBER 28

How difficult it is to paint eyes that do not appeal to the spectator. How difficult to think more of Laszlo's life than his death.

OCTOBER 10

I test every passage of the painting as if it were a lie on the convincingness of which my life depended. I write lie and not truth because we do not test the truth so vigorously unless it is a new truth, and if it is that, it will first appear to be a lie. Further, I have a conscience about each passage, just as if it were a lie. It haunts me, leaps back at me when I have forgotten it, nags at me, destroys my interest in anything else, until finally I make it believable – even sometimes true.

OCTOBER 29

Colour can hide a form; it must never be allowed to. Colour can be applied – like lipstick – and that is fatal. Most white rose buds are red to begin with. At the moment of opening, when the form of the rose is disclosed, at that very moment the petals which constitute that form are seen to be – white. So it must be with a form in a painting. The form and the colour must disclose each other simultaneously. The first light that, falling upon a form, first discloses it, does so by means of the form's colour. I with all my breadth and range of choice, with my 5-foot painting table with my colours on it, must in the end achieve an inevitability of colour comparable to that of the white rose as it opens.

NOVEMBER 6

Several bad days and bad light. The row of feet at the bottom are a bore: too many white laces. Suddenly the whole conception strikes me as trivial. Of course it is better painting than most, but that is a quite irrelevant judgement. John is always coming in after he has been round the galleries, indignant and furious about what he has seen. It's a betrayal, he says between his teeth. But I can get no more angry about bad painting by people who are not painters than I can about the price of fish.

This painting seems trivial only in terms of what it might be, of what I might paint. Today every painter worthy of the name is his own master, his own pupil and perhaps finally his own debaser, his own mannerist. We each have to decide everything for ourselves. We each have to *choose* what is inconceivable for us. As artists – and this is the curse that is upon us – we must each visualize our own city, ourself as its centre. It is bitter for me to admit this, I who, as a man, believe in the collective, in the revolutionary class not the revolutionary individual.

But art is the most inconvenient of activities, the least susceptible to will or legislation. It is always forward or backward in its desires, defying the present. It is like a flame. It is governed and fed by the present wind; but it is always trying to flicker under the wind, to lick the wind off from its source. Without the wind, without air, the flame would not exist. But the stronger the wind the firmer the grip of the flame on its object, and the swifter its attempts to undercut the wind. We can take over the means of production; but we cannot altogether take over the means of expression. Thus I remain lonely, holding no brief for loneliness. Thus sometimes I question my own choice. Sometimes, such as tonight, I look at my city, the way of life that my art presupposes, with incredulity. I stare at it like a peasant from the countryside. All the courage and debris, wounds, last hours and struggles that I have seen – Katinka, Carlo, Erhardt, Yvonne, Ernst, Laci – do they truly find their expression in these clear colours and untroubled forms? Is this what we shall come to?

NOVEMBER 10

Give me the ease with figures that sailors have with ropes – to coil them through space, to make them fast, to join them together. Sometimes if I have dreamt well, I have it.

NOVEMBER 19

To be free of this slave-driving necessity to work. Is that why I strive to finish – in the illusory hope that it will be the end; that after this canvas I will lie in the sun and be blind for a week?

NOVEMBER 20

The athletes are not acrobats. It is news not entertainment that they bring.

DECEMBER 15

It is weeks since I have written anything. Now I only want to record – so as to remind myself later when this stage has been passed – that today I consider this the best painting I have yet achieved.

DECEMBER 26

The colours must be louder.
Diana is out with friends and I have the stadium to myself. I look at the canvas. It is dead. I have overreached myself. I should stick to etching plates. Yet I am old enough to know that this is not true. The painting is not so different from when I wrote what I did a week ago. And in a week's time? I know my

133

own history, and I can sit by my own sick bed waiting for myself to recover. But the canvas there – that fifth wall to the studio – still remains offensive to both invalid and watcher. I shall drape something over it until a recovery has been made. I have lived in the athlete's stadium for months, I need a change. The forms are like words repeated until they become meaningless.

The business of painting – of making the shit fit your vision – was always difficult, as I never tire of reminding myself. But perhaps the sense of defeat now comes about in a different way – when it does come. Today every painter *pleads* with the spectator – come, come; look, look; see it! But once, as in a paper-chase, the trail the painter had laid was clear. He still had to train himself. He still had to run like Zatopek. But he never had to pause to look back. Whereas we must do so constantly. We have no confetti in a bag to throw behind us because we have no tradition. And so we are always stopping to see whether we are lost, to check whether the path we've come along is a path at all. And that stopping and starting saps our stamina. Tonight this huge canvas is like a flat wall, informing me that I have come to a dead end. I have no energy to go farther, for I can find no incentive in what I can see there on the canvas. Only misconstruction. The painting itself is blind. Undyed linen is more beautiful.

I have been out to the pub to regain my sense. Any talk soon makes nonsense of monologues. There was a North Countryman at the bar: a bald man of about sixty with an artful face, a male fortune-teller's. He was telling story after story to the gang around him, but the smile he was working for was the barmaid's. I beat him there. One of his stories I liked particularly. Once he had fallen out, he said, with the local policeman – an officious bastard always poking his nose in and hopping around like a blue-arsed fly. And at that time, he said, he had just acquired a dog. The policeman tried to charge him for not putting a collar on this dog. In fact, he warned him three times. And so, in the end, said the man at the bar, I bought a collar, and after that the bastard kept out of my way. On the collar he had had printed: I'm Joe Furlong's dog. Whose are you? The canvas is still a farce. The dog joke is better.

1955

It goes better. It looked like the laundry in a washing-machine
because the colours were too broken up. A little red, a little blue,
a little green – embroidery on an apron. But now the colours
come down on the forms like waves. Each front figure is the
same colour as its frieze-figure partner behind. Only the thick-
ness of line and the shadows on the limb are different. It is
coming. The forms, which are also limbs, begin to entice, my
eyes embark. Yet it must be much clearer yet. Everything must
be made blatant, and then if it looks commonplace we know
where we are.

FEBRUARY 10

At times failure is very necessary for the artist. It reminds him
that a failure is not the ultimate disaster. And this reminder
liberates him from the mean fussing of perfectionism.

*The outward evidence of Janos's moods at this time was very
undramatic. On occasions he appeared slightly disheartened, and
then he would try to distract my attention away from 'the fifth
wall' of the studio and show me some small canvas he had raked out
and perhaps re-worked; on other occasions he was obviously somewhat pleased, and quizzing the huge canvas would say, 'Yes. Yes.
It begins to count. No?'*

*Sometimes we used to go out for the evening together to the
cinema or to the Hancocks' to look at their television. As we walked
home past the dreary little shops of the Fulham Road, Janos fell
silent and began to walk a little more quickly, an expression of
irritable preoccupied determination on his face which forced whoever
was with him to lag behind and walk by themselves. He was always
the first to stride down the dimly lit, stone, basement-like passage of
the studios, hurrying like a man taken short. By the time we had got
into the studio he had disappeared. He was on the other side of the
canvas. A few moments later he would join us round the stove,
looking markedly relieved or much worse. If worse, he would say
nothing but only smoke, drink coffee and look at the paint-stained
floor. He also became very sensitive to praise for other artists of his*

own generation. For example, I once started talking enthusiastically about Gonzalez, whom I knew he had known and admired. I could see he didn't like it. His face froze. Yet this was not a question of jealousy – as his own entry about Gonzalez proves. At such times he simply did not know how to judge himself, and so hated to be reminded of the standards of any kind of equivalent judgement.

Another sign of his interior strain was his absolute refusal to leave London. Both Diana and I tried several times, for one reason or another, to persuade him to go away for two or three days. He was adamant. His frown would consolidate, his hand would grip the table or the back of the chair, he would draw himself out of his stoop – ' You may not think of it. But I have work to do. W O R K. You understand?'

Although a break of a couple of days could only have helped him, he was obsessively frightened of leaving the canvas until he had it in a state with which he was satisfied.

FEBRUARY 24

What a wickedly grand proscenium arch the ego erects, so that we are saved from the bother of even having to disguise our trivialities. Worked all day in the stadium. It goes slowly.

MARCH 7

Diana has 'flu and is in bed with a high temperature. Her sub-missiveness reminds me of how she sometimes was in her early twenties. The reminder makes our quarrelling seem intolerably sordid, and guilt overwhelms me. I nurse her and do not work much. Max and the Hancocks come round to see her. Max has a marvellous sickroom manner. He has the air of having been through so much himself that he is automatically reassuring to any patient, however ill. I am not satisfied with the group lifting up the victor. Not enough air through it. Too much mass.

MARCH 10

I am a bad husband. Have worked more on the group, which is opening out and getting better.

MARCH 14

Twist the back of the extreme left-hand figure. What eyes

Cubism has given us! Never again can we make a painting of a single view. We now have a visual dialectic. How easy it should be for Marxists to understand! But these days I stick to my own magnificent problems – how to paint the armoured knee-cap and the valley of the back of the knee side by side to represent one leg. Magnificent because so difficult.

MARCH 25

There comes a time in every work when suddenly the form of it takes over. Then I can do no wrong. I am Adam in paradise. And the whole of life seems to have conspired to help me. It can last five minutes. Just occasionally, like today, for a whole afternoon.

APRIL 6

Diana is better, but she needs a rest. I suggested to her she should have a holiday. I doubt if she will. As I work, I hear her moving about the other side of the canvas and, No, let it sleep.

Diana did go away for a few days – with me. I had to go to an Arts Festival in Amsterdam and, at Janos's suggestion, I persuaded her to come with me. It was a revealing experience. I had not previously realized how much she had absorbed of Janos's way of life. When I saw them together I was always most aware of their differences. Yet during the first day in Amsterdam I suddenly saw how similar Diana's reactions were to what Janos's would have been. She was suspicious of the international art experts we saw gathered in the hotel vestibule. 'They look like bloody jewellers,' she said. She chose to drink in the shabbier cafés and, like Janos, sat if possible in a corner facing the door to examine everyone who came in. She ate herrings raw and wanted to hire a bicycle. Only on the last evening when there was a reception and dance for the special guests of the Festival was she transformed back to her true character. I introduced her to some museum officials, and suddenly she was away – dancing, asking questions, laughing, drinking champagne. 'John,' she said, coming up to me a little tight, 'who is that important-looking man over there with silver hair?' I did not know. But a little later she was dancing with him. Furthermore, with her transformation – or, perhaps more accurately, liberation of manner – her appearance changed. With her hair up and in her evening dress, it was indeed hard to recognize the woman with the dispatch-case trudging to the Municipal Library. Even her habitual tension of movement was transformed into a kind of sharp vivacity. I wished that Janos could have seen her; but that could never have been possible.

APRIL 16

The studio without Diana makes me feel older. Waking up in the middle of the night and knowing that I have the place to myself reminds me of Berlin thirty years ago. And the contrast between my preoccupations then and now makes me feel all my age. Then there were a hundred ways of proving oneself; now there is only one.

APRIL 18

Leonard Gough asked if he could come round to see my work. His disability makes him very direct. When he came through the door he saw the back of the canvas and straightway pulled out the pad from his pocket and, writing upside down so that I could read the message immediately, wrote, A MINIATURIST! He is an old-fashioned man, a Dickensian. In front of the canvas, his hat still on, he looked it up and down and sideways, as though searching for a door in a wall. Then he stepped back and lit his pipe and waited – as if now he expected the canvas to move off like a bus. But all the time he was watching rather slyly, and I saw him beginning to smile. After several minutes he took out his pad. MAY I OFFER YOU MY HEARTFELT CONGRATU-LATIONS? He handed me his tobacco pouch, and I took an old pipe of mine that I hadn't used for years and filled it. We stood there smoking, and Gough showed me with his hands what he liked in *The Games*. His only criticism was that some of the contours of the figures on the wall should be filled in solid, so as to relate them more closely in weight to the figures in front. He is probably right about this. After he had gone, I found a scrap of paper on the floor. It was the page on which he had offered me his congratulations.

APRIL 19

This interminable fiddling. I cannot even walk as a painter.

APRIL 21

For a few hours after Diana came back, she seemed to have all the buoyancy that she had fifteen years ago.

APRIL 28

Obscurely, I feel a need to defend myself. Generalizations are *not* formalism. I know it. Generalizations stand in for hundreds of particulars. Formalism is a huge temptation. We live in an almost closed world of art, and formalism is art which gets over its problems without a glance at anything outside itself. The formalist work is self-sufficient. It is a commodity. The market for such commodities is made up of those who believe that they also are self-sufficient – members of the mincing cosmopolitan art world.

Cosmopolitanism and formalism feed together. As soon as you wrench pictures out of their context, and – more important still – imagine that they have none, you will start thinking that generalizations or justified simplifications are formalizations. Look at the nonsense written about Cézanne. He's an abstracting theoretician only so long as you forget Provence and ignore that saint of mountains. Then you see that he was doing the same thing as Chardin: looking at nature so hard that his gaze began to revolve it, like a stream a mill wheel. Or Piero della Francesca. His skies and hills look sublime in London. In Umbria they are less extraordinary than buses. My athletes are all the heroes I have known, now made victorious. They come to meet me, I who am still fighting and am no hero. Yet how Bill Neale would question this! What's their victory? he would demand. Are they working-class athletes who have been given their chance by Socialism? They could be that for Bill.

Yet in my painting their victory consists of the way in which they have been painted. Their arrangement, the energy of their forms, the way my colour reveals them – that is their victory. Somewhere David wrote: 'I am going to paint some soldiers, calm before the battle, promising themselves immortality.' But

139

in a painting such immortality can only be promised by the visual dignity and vigour of the painting itself. Does that contradict what I have just written about formalism? It should not, for that is where Bill, with his emphasis on the connexion between art and events, is more than half right. We must purify reality; we cannot create our own substitute for it. Where Bill is wrong is that we never paint a single event – even if our title suggests that we do. On every canvas I paint another climax of my whole life experience. I am a painter and not a writer or a politician or a lover because I recognize a climax in the way two hanging cherries touch one another or in the structural difference between a horse's leg and a man's leg. Who can understand that?

The truth is that to people like Bill the Party is a kind of work of art in itself. All his creativity, all his imagination is centred on the Party. And therefore all other art strikes him as somewhat frivolous. He would never admit this, of course. But you can see it in the way he looks round the studio, the way he comes in – an oracle in a mac. He came in the other day and he looked at *The Games* canvas – as if it were the most eccentric piece of washing hanging out to dry. He is like a man behind the lines on leave – restless, hard-pressed and all of whose nervous energy is transferred into action. He is unflinching and his courage makes him generous. When he leaves, he grips my hand and says, 'Good luck.' But what he might say more truthfully is, 'We're struggling for your right to potter about here, too, you know. Carry on. But of course we may need you later.' To which my reply ought to be certain: 'You will need me when you understand the inspiration of my paintings.'

MAY DAY
Every good painting has a pendulum swinging in it.

MAY 21
Watched *The Games* all day, preparing to take the largest risk. The soft blacks must now become jet blacks. Printer's ink. Then the numerals and the black trunks and the outlines and the running shoes and the netting will print themselves on the rest of the painting – like a tattoo on a strong shoulder. It is May

Day, 1955. Late. Late. But to me it still seems a beginning.

MAY 23

The blacks work. Everything is now clamped down.

JUNE 18

The Games is finished. It has taken me eleven months. Tonight we moved it to the side of the studio. A strange picture we must have presented. A man and his wife at either end of a wall of canvas, shouting directions to one another, and the canvas swaying and in danger of toppling over. But we got it to the wall safely. Now that it is there, it looks quite different. It looks much larger again – like a flag unfurled indoors. It has its idiosyncrasies, which I regret. But I can do nothing about them. They are locked now, like everything else in it, in a chain of cause and effect. On the whole, it is a strong chain: A Good Painting. I am happy.

JULY 7

Hancock, gazing at *The Games*, said, 'It's very gay. Reminds me of a roundabout at a fair.' Then he thought this comparison tactless and looking confused added, 'Of course it is a quite different thing.' I reassured him and told him I wanted it to be gay. 'Too true,' he said as he always does, 'Too true, but no one else could have done it quite like you have.'

Tonight, instead of talking at the café because there exists neither the kind of café nor the kind of talk I have in mind, I wonder about this canvas that is now finished, that stands now in its own right. When I have finished a work, I always want to get drunk. If I did not live so fortunately and so isolatedly in England, I doubt whether I would ever write these notes. What I find myself thinking as a result of writing them would go into talk, and, when my friends were away, into letters. No painter wants to frame his canvases in words. *The Games* is there for the time when people will look at it.

I fill in the time. Only very seldom can we be certain what any one of our works communicates. So much lies behind each one. It is impossible for me to know exactly what *The Games* will mean for others. Anyway this will change. What is most striking about it today may seem irrelevant in twenty years' time. This abundance of the artist's intentions is what makes the problem of propaganda so complicated. Nevertheless, it is *the* problem of art in our time.

There is one thing about myself of which I am sure: I am a modern painter, and I am so because I have lived all my life with the problem of propaganda – the problem of facing other men as a man. I would like to write about this some time. I know about it. But now we are going to the cinema.

JULY 8

There are three ways in which an artist can fight for what he believes:

(1) With a gun or stone. Laszlo talked of the streets cobbled with gold for the demonstrators because from the cobbled streets we could always grub up stones to throw.

(2) By putting his skill at the service of the immediate propagandists – by producing cartoons, emblems, posters, slogans.

(3) By producing works entirely on his own volition. By working under circumstances in which neither the enemy police nor the enemy troops nor his own edit. prop. prompt his actions, but in which the no-less-strong force he works under is his own inner tension.

Each of these ways is justified depending on the situation the man is in.

Like all 1, 2, 3 divisions, this is somewhat over-simplified. The compartments are not exclusive.

I have seen a poet, fighting with stones, declaiming his own verses. And I have seen the same poet's head smashed like earthenware by the hooves of the Emperor's cavalry. A painter, listening to the instructions of his edit. prop. can find that these are identical with the instructions of his own personal vision. An artist working under his own volition can even sometimes produce works which supply slogans or emblems for the street corners – Picasso and Brecht.

Still. Roughly there are three separate ways in which we can fight for what we believe, and the way we fight depends upon the situation in which we find ourselves. The ways of the gun and the emergency editorial committee are usually short-lived. In a way, of course, there is always an emergency. Have my political comrades ever lived through anything else? But if a man is forced or chooses to meet continually the direct demands of one emergency after another, he ceases to be primarily an artist. It is not shameful to cease to be an artist – such an idea only comes from the melancholy of romanticism. When the English Hogarth said that he would rather rid London of cruelty than paint the Sistine chapel, he was making a more than reasonable choice.

Yet those who do remain artists working under their own volition – how do we fight for what we believe? In what way are we militant? The very question would sound absurd to most of my fellow painters in London. We are not militant, they would say: and if they were honest they would add that they paint to make money or to discover something about themselves. Or – most likely of all – just because they enjoy it. Who could object? But let there be no deception. This is not why Delacroix, Géricault, Courbet, Cézanne, Pissarro, Van Gogh, Gauguin worked; nor is it why any other major artist of the last two centuries worked. All of these men were militant: militant to the point of being prepared to die for what they believed in. Delacroix believed in what he called 'the beautiful'; Cézanne in his *petite sensation;* Van Gogh in his 'Humanity, humanity, and again humanity'. They fought for their various visions and most of their militant energy was concerned with fighting the difficulties of realizing their vision, of finding the visual forms that would turn their hunches into facts. Each of their different visions, however, sprang from the same kind of conviction; they each knew that life could be better, richer, juster, truer than it was. Every modern attempt to create a work of art is based on the desire (usually undeclared) to increase the value of the experience that gave rise to the work. In the nineteenth and twentieth centuries such an increase in *value* must inevitably be counted in terms of human pleasure, truth or justice. Earlier maybe it was different. Cézanne stared at the Mont St Victoire in order to add to the truth that was knowable by the human intellect and senses. What most aesthetes forget is that their pleasurable inquiries and sensations only begin to be pleasurable given a certain standard of comfort, and that, for one reason or another, most modern artists have lived beneath that standard. You do not notice the difference between good and indifferent wine on a very empty stomach.

I can see the moon through the skylight, and somewhere there is an owl. It is surprising how many owls there are in London. Writing as I have done makes me nostalgic. Why do the lights on the Erzebet Bridge still flicker for me, whilst the recollection of sailing under it, lying on my back on the bottom of a dinghy, leaves me only incredulous about the way I lived then? Why do the lights on the Erzebet Bridge still flicker for me? The bridge has been destroyed, anyway.

JULY 10

The modern artist fights to contribute to human happiness, truth or justice. He works to improve the world.

Let no one be deceived by the detached beauty of their works as they now hang safe in the museums – this was their aim, and there is not one modern artist of stature who has not declared it in so many words. So art is just a question of good intentions and the great artist the man with the best intentions? Again I hear the sceptic's questioning encouraged by the amoral limbo in which we live, and where any attempt to connect art with social responsibility and morality is immediately ridiculed by parody. Again the answer is No. There are many writers and painters who do not wish to improve the world, but only to amuse or justify themselves: such men are not artists. There are others who long to improve the human condition, but who, in terms of their own art, have little to contribute. Such men reproduce the discoveries of others or, carried away by their fervour, express their sentiments without proving them.

Sentimental works are ones which have never really been begun, which embody only the hope instead of the discovery. The important artist actually sees how he can improve the world. God knows it's a small improvement when it strikes him. The originality of any artist is very slight. And let us be clear what improvement means. It has nothing to do with moralizing. A red-chalk drawing of a torso is not going to discourage adultery – it may even encourage it. Katinka had the most beautiful back I have ever seen. For the artist the improvement is largely a matter

144

of greater accuracy, in telling the truth as he sees it. The consequences of that truth being told, the often tangible and practical improvements that follow it – he can usually only guess at. All Cézanne could do was to be faithful to his *petite sensation*. Yet, when he was about five years older than I am now, he knew it meant more than that and he said, 'I am beginning to enter the promised land; shall I be like Moses or shall I be able to enter it?' Now every good modern building that is put up owes something to his *petite sensation*.

The artist inherits from his infancy or his ancestors an expectation of life and working human kindness which is contradicted by his later experience of the real world. I was going to be the finest horseman of the Hortobagy. Up to this point he is like lots of delinquents and criminals. What makes him an artist is the use to which he puts his disappointment – his discontent. First he finds within his medium the equivalent of the qualities he feels to be lacking in life. Every formal quality has its emotional equivalent. Then he begins the endless task of trying to interpret reality with these qualities always inherent in his interpretation. Perhaps no one but an artist can quite understand this. Yet it is the fundamental way in which we set out to to improve the world. It is only a subjective improvement? No, because a true work of art communicates and so extends consciousness of what is possible.

I have taught all day today and I am too tired to write more. I shall show these last few notes to J. It might even be useful to publish them as an article.

He never did show them to me. And although obviously these pages are argued in the kind of way that suggests Janos had public readers in mind, I now believe in the light of later events that he was really arguing with his own conscience. To me, despite all the differences, this journal reads at times like Gauguin's in Tahiti. Both men were too strong to be nostalgic. But both were haunted by their exile from where they could be known for what they were.

JULY 12

As Communists we believe that we understand how, on a far

more urgent and immediate level, we can make life better, richer, juster, truer with a speed that has never been possible before. I believe this despite the harshness, the treachery, the deaths. I believe it with Asia and Africa, for whom such an improvement is life and death for their own and the next generation. The point from which politics starts for me is hunger. Nothing less.

Yet life does not end with bread and medical supplies – even though the majority in this fortunate country forget that it begins with them. It extends to the subtlest calculations that lay behind the rendering of Cézanne's *petite sensation*. And so, when once we have realized how the true artist is a militant improver, we must welcome him as an ally. It is possible that we may have a better understanding than him of how the improvement of life for which he works and longs can be realized economically, socially, administratively. It is even possible that his personal political opinions and the superficial content of his work will be opposed to the political measures we believe to be necessary. Yet still we must recognize that *any* extension of the range of human imagination is a contribution to our own aim. Now I hear my old teachers arguing. And the class struggle? And our Marxist understanding of the connexion between the superstructure of art and the economic basis? Comrade Lavin, they ask, Have you accepted the comfortable illusions of the bourgeoisie with whom you have surrounded yourself? I have not. But I believe that we have made a profound mistake whenever we have used our Marxism to make an arbitrary division between art that is for us (progressive art) and art which is against us (decadent art). All good art is for Man – and therefore for us. The division we should make is between good art and bad art. To judge between the good and the bad is a difficult task, but we are far better equipped for it than the bourgeoisie because we have learnt the lessons of history better – including art history. During the last eighty years every innovation and discovery in art has shocked the bourgeois. They should never shock us if we pride ourselves on understanding how consciousness is developed and conditioned; yet innovations have shocked us and we have denied them. The bourgeoisie fear the truth. But we have feared lies and in our fear have created them.

Reading back over the last few pages, the old questions pound again in my head. They are asked by those who, unlike me, bear heavy responsibilities.

Have you not been out of the struggle too long? No. My whole point is that I have never left the struggle. My contribution has been very small, but it is dangerous to try to make it bigger. Do not demand a Socialist Art. Many do, but they haven't the slightest idea what they are asking for. Demand Socialist propaganda when it is needed and encourage art. Then artists will suddenly realize that they have created Socialist works, whilst only thinking about the truth.

You assume a degree of rational consciousness among people that does not yet exist – don't you realize that bad art of a reactionary character can mislead and corrupt the people? Only if they are already disillusioned, for bad art deals in illusions. If the people are already disillusioned – find the causes for it and change them. Then 'the dangerous art' will be rendered harmless.

You play only with words. Instead of the words progressive and decadent, you substitute good and bad. What have you changed? Very little, because neither I nor anyone else can supply a true formula for creating or judging art. But a false formula and a cult are more likely to attach themselves to the words progressive and decadent than to the words good and bad.

Do you now deny that art has a class basis? Of course not. The sickening futility of so much contemporary art in the West can only be explained in terms of the ideological disintegration of the bourgeoisie. A kind of class paranoia has set in. The cult of irrationalism and fear is in the last analysis a result of a class fear of Socialism. But need the work of artists who are Socialists reflect an equal but different kind of fear – a fear of obscurity like the child's fear of the darkness?

You deny the possibility of a Socialist, popular art? No. It will come. But it cannot be demanded. Do not ask for Socialist works of art to be judged by Socialist standards. The standards will be untrue and opportunist. Instead, turn artists into Communists. The problem centres on the man, not the work.

Of course a desire to improve the world is not in itself worth

147

much. Of course one must add, How? And improvement for whom? And as soon as I try to answer those questions I realize that organization and discipline are necessary, as well as an understanding of history. Marxism and the Party provide this organization, discipline and understanding. *But for the artist so can his art.* Finally, there should be no contradictions between the discipline of Communism and the discipline of art; the more artists there are who are Communists the less there will be. But at the moment contradiction can arise. And we must live with it. Every attempt to turn an artist into a politician increases the contradiction. The more he understands his political significance as an artist – not as a politician – the less the contradiction will be.

You think and talk all the time about the artist. What of the people, the working class, whom he should serve? I believe in the greatest potentiality of their talent and understanding. But I cannot serve like a waiter. We live in a period of transition – transition to Socialism, transition to Communism. Our historical understanding is enabling us to change the world. For the first time in history we – scientific Socialists – can take our standards from the future we are creating. But I cannot, as an artist, work by the light of an historical principle. I must work by the light of my senses – here and now. For an artist there is no such thing as a period of transition. *He faces his subject as if it were timeless.* How much has been lost by this simple fact not being understood? Even in a period of transition men grow old and die and children are born. The politician can sometimes forget this. I never.

AUGUST II

I have glimpsed how pictures can be cherished. One of the students at the School is a Cypriot. Very earnest, very proud, trying to make two moments out of every one of his education, and very likeable. All last term he was trying to persuade me to go and see the works of a friend of his, another Cypriot painter. I went today. This friend lives with his aunt, who keeps a café, in two rooms in Camden Town. After I'd seen the boy's paintings, the aunt insisted upon my having tea. Tea being Cypriot wine, olives, salami and God knows what else. Mediterranean hospitality in the grimness of Camden Town. She is a short woman, bag-shaped, and always, I imagine, dressed in her traditional peasant black. Her eyes are withdrawn, only they are made sharp by a squint. While I ate, she stood at one side of the table, and whenever I looked at her, she smiled and propelled herself towards me behind her huge bosom to offer me another plate of something to eat. After the meal was over, she said, 'Now, mister, would you like to see my pictures?' I was surprised because I found it hard to believe that she painted as well. Then it turned out that I had misunderstood her. What she wanted to show me were her photographs and snapshots of Cyprus. Yet, in fact, I had not entirely misunderstood her, because for her there was absolutely no distinction between her photographs and her nephew's paintings – many of which were also of Cypriot scenes. How could there be? Both transported her home, and when she was there, she was not going to bother about exactly what kind of vessel it was she had sailed in. She held each picture up in front of her, before giving it to me, as if it were a mirror. Here was her son, proudly sporting an American tie. Now, she said, he only had one arm. How did that happen? He was shot. She said it with ancient weariness – as if it were a time-honoured blasphemy that had retained its meaning but could no longer shock. Behind her large bosom, behind her smile, behind her counter in the café downstairs, she had lived now for a long time with the image of an arm severed off from her son and thrown into a bin. But I don't think it occurred to her that the shot might have been fired by the son of one of her British customers. Here was the house he had been born in – with a protruding roof to give shade to the ground on one side of it. Here was an old photographer's photograph of her husband. In ceremonial sepia. He was drowned. Here were her friends. Here was the bay you could see from the house. Here were her nieces bathing. Here was the bought postcard of the church. That is where she was married. Here was her brother in the door of his shop. At the end, she kept her stubby thumb pressed hard down on the last photograph. I leant over to look at it, for I knew surely that it was of her. Here was a young girl, and as I studied it she straightened her back with pride and smiled. She was proud in the same way as if it had been her daughter. And, by the same token, I smiled at her as if I were going to be her future son-in-law. When she gathered the photographs up, she placed them in a leather wallet under some brightly embroidered, treasured garment.

I have never seen drawings handled as those photographs were handled. And no museum in the world contains for its curator such treasures as that tallboy's drawer for Mme Michaelis. Let all painters here face the challenge of that fact. Myself among them.

AUGUST 19

This journal records too many deaths. Now it is Léger's. He was the greatest artist of our time. He will not only live, he will father an art.

AUGUST 23

With *The Games* finished, I am temporarily at a loss. Began a painting of Susan. I would like to die painting a nude. There is so much to disclose with pleasure. Our eyes are like hands, searching in the dark for fruit, a head of hair, breasts, a perfect sphere, another hand, a window which opened will let in the air from a night landscape; only the dark we search in is the white of our paper or canvas. Maybe it is for this reason that we see as differently from other people, as the blind feel. We seize on the essentials so as not to be deceived. We know how easily dogs can slip their collars, women their rings or – as how well I know it – men their countries. I have just looked again at the canvas. It is not bad.

SEPTEMBER 2

The crowds in the Battersea Gardens. Figures in relation to trees: idling along their walks, ski-ing between them, placing ladders against them to pick their fruit, training them as we train the vines on our red hills, felling them. Myself gathering sticks for the fire on my uncle's farm. Man and wood. Yet as I watch the crowds in the Battersea Gardens, I see the trees there as almost man-made objects – just as the horses on the round-abouts are man-made. It could have been a new canvas by Léger who is now dead. I must alter the victor's left leg. It is a little weak.

SEPTEMBER 7

Today I was honoured. I have reached the time of life for honours. This is one which, had I known about it in advance, I would not have refused. It was George Trent's private view. Looking back on it, I now see why George was so insistent that I should go. June met me at the door and kissed me. A pleasurable honour in itself. The place was full of people, but since it is his first show many of them were students and other painter friends. The cuckoos do not yet know of his nest. The largest painting on a wall by itself was new to me. A mother and child in a chair. I opened the catalogue to see when he had painted it. It had no title. It read – No. 15. *In Homage to Janos Lavin, Painter.* I looked for George. It was a beautiful gesture. You taught me most of what I know, he said, when I found him. I have corrected the leg.

Janos came up to George, red-faced and obviously very excited. When, however, he was particularly moved or felt particularly affectionate, Janos had the habit of half-slapping the other person's cheek. So he now slapped George's face, and George, equally brusque in his North Country manner, punched Janos in the chest. A distant spectator might have thought a brawl was starting. Then they stood apart, laughing like boys. Yet George was clearly a little anxious about whether Janos really liked the painting.

'*You do think it's come off?*' *he said.*

'*The mother's left arm does not quite go into the sleeve. Otherwise it is very, very good,*' *said Janos.*

SEPTEMBER 25

Last week I began a new canvas. The profiles of two men against the night. The night regular as blue serge. Worked on it most of the day. But early I went out.

Every fine Sunday the cyclists speed down the Fulham Road on their way out of the city. If it is sunny, I stroll along simply to watch them. Today I met Mrs Hancock. She had obviously been crying. I walked with her, but asked nothing. She walks like a good mare. She explained. Len had persuaded another woman to pose for him, and was going to be painting her all day. I took her to a coffee-house at South Kensington, and tried to explain to her that this was not necessarily an act of unfaithfulness, and suggested that if she showed herself a little more willing to pose for Len she could beat any competitor. This last she took as a pass at her on my part, looking down with her eyes and playing with one of her earrings. She was wearing a pale blue linen dress, her arms as beautiful as pale honey-coloured wood. In every city there are millions of places of revelation. I can remember thinking in Berlin in 1933 how strange it was that girls' ears were still so delicate. I explained to her how she must entice Len and take it all more light-heartedly. She listened to what I had to say like a child listening to a school-teacher enumerating the unseeable capitals of the world. Stockholm, Sofia, Copenhagen, Budapest . . . names somehow to be remembered and coupled with the right country. I could only have shown her what I meant by making love to her.

OCTOBER 10

Has any sculptor ever modelled a figure on a real bicycle as base? I believe it would be possible. The figure in beaten silver alloy: the front wheel of the bicycle off the ground. Unhappily most sculptors here are more interested in Etruria, dead two thousand years. I do not want a public with great aesthetic sensibility. I want a public with one thing – hope. A profile eye is a formidable problem.

OCTOBER 18

I have scraped down most of the two heads. Problem: how to bring into contrast a pink face and the forest dark of the sky, how to paint neon light. Bad day.

OCTOBER 25

It is a strange solitude that we choose. Yet we do choose it so there is no point whatsoever in regretting it. It is like the solitude of a man who, for some reason, is able to see all the stars in the sky in the daylight. The other people in the street stare at him as he looks up at the sky, and then they look up themselves because they believe he can see an aeroplane. Which quite possibly he can. But it wasn't why he was looking.

Every time I come back here I look over at *The Games*. I did something there. I brought it out. Diana looks at it and sees committees, and not the flowers which are in it but the flowers which will be put in front of it when it's in ceremonial position. The man who collects the shillings from the gas-meter looks at it and sees a lot of figures made of triangles and bunting. He may or may not like it. He should be given time. The one thing painting needs – TIME. And Peace is time. But, anyway, he has few preconceived ideas, and obviously it is a big job of work. He hasn't that sneaking, suspicious feeling, which the bourgeois can never lose, that I may be laughing at him. He can laugh as well as I can.

Nevertheless, what I see is like the stars in daylight. In every shape on that canvas I could now go to sleep happy. None of it is just paint now, just coloured shit. It is clean. Every colour has ceased to be something that can be rubbed off. Has become space and form. No one else will ever quite understand the satisfaction of that. The painted athletes will take the credit. Which is right. The content of the picture must always get the credit of the painter's technical struggle. The great acrobat, the great juggler, the great comedian, always appears to be giving his performance for the first time, because when you look at his performance it is inconceivable that there should have been any struggle. The performance must take all, leaving us only our names. Painter and critics always mean something different by the word style. Critics mean panache, elegance. But when I say *The Games* has style, I simply mean I see the best of myself in it. And this best is almost impersonal because it is quite separate from myself as I am.

OCTOBER 26

Would you have understood what I wrote last night? You sacrificed too much, Laci. Cézanne: *L'état c'est nous: la peinture c'est moi*. We cannot sacrifice ourselves and remain artists. When working we have to believe *la peinture c'est moi*. It is not. But we have to believe it. And when I say that, is it so dangerous? If I had knocked on your door and whispered, *C'est moi*, you would not have been alarmed. You would have thought Jansci. Or if you had to explain to a comrade with you who it was, you would have whispered: Janos Lavin, alias Wolfgang Weber, Budapest

1919, Berlin till 1933, inroad chain, anti-Fascist painter, safe. Is it then so dangerous that when working I say *la peinture c'est moi*? I am the same man.

Must we now, as shamefully contrite old men, denounce all the 'decadence' of our youth when we believed in a spontaneously revolutionary art? We shall look like a concourse of undertakers. We were instructed to bury subjectivism. But in the coffin without our knowing it is one of our instructors, my friend as a brother, Laci.

In the name of our strength could it not be a wedding instead? The marriage between the life-long struggle towards a language of form and the life-long struggle as a Communist. Those spaces and forms and all the neatness of their coincidences – neat as sex – I have not struggled over them half my life to make them for their own sake. I can only work with a sense of direction. I must know in which direction to search. I must know for what I am longing. Otherwise I would only make pure circles and spheres.

Here I sought a connexion between bodies that was entirely free, the result of an entirely voluntary contract, liberated even from gravity. Here I sought dignity – a body doing what it can do well. Here I sought strength – expressing itself in a combination of action and ease. Here also I sought happiness – the result of making a harmony of the whole. Unnatural words maybe, because words cannot define the satisfaction we seek. Words are better for protesting.

Yet when I work with my forms that have come from a man and will become a man again, but will make this new, unique, painted man, free, dignified, strong, happy, I am working from my conviction that living men can similarly transform themselves by transforming their own society into a classless one. If I paint a capable hand, a noble head, a group of figures moving together, they have come from the proletariat even though they are without recognizable emblems. Even those who believe in God cannot paint confident paintings in Europe today. Only we.

You look incredulous? But you sacrificed too much. In the end perhaps the sacrifice broke you. All that you denied of yourself – perhaps in the end all this took revenge on you. A repressed artist is the most dangerous of men, much given to treachery, hideous illusions and destruction. What became of you, my friend as a brother?

NOVEMBER 1

Self-knowledge – the knowledge of one's own motives and needs – must always be balanced by an equal degree of world knowledge – that is to say, objective knowledge of nature, society, environment, other people. It is this balance – not necessarily the amount of knowledge on either side, that is the quality that leads to people being called wise. If the balance is unequal – too much self-knowledge produces the anarchist, and too much world knowledge the bureaucrat.

NOVEMBER 2

Last night I had a great surprise. John and the Hancocks were here and suddenly there was a knock on the door. I went to open it – and there was Michel. I knew he was holding an exhibition in London, but had never dreamt he would come over for it, let alone look me up after twenty years.

He said I looked the same as ever. He was greatly changed. I recognized him immediately, but as you still recognize a landscape that has been transformed by building. He is a figure of success. He was always in the news twenty years ago. But now he gives interviews to young journalists. Not what he does, but what he says, is news now. It is as if all his natural characteristics have been carefully, unnaturally preserved. His curly hair is now like a grey wig. And all his nervous energy and passion, which once made people shake their heads and think of terrible love affairs or suicide, has now become a kind of tip-toe sprightliness; he is now like a clown standing on a large, brightly coloured ball. Only his generosity is the same. But a loveable man.

The whole evening I tried to picture us as we had lived in Paris, and I found it impossible. Only affection remained. Over the sumptuous dinner he gave us, I tried to visualize us sitting in the Rue Saint Jacques. I could not. It is far easier to do so, sitting here alone in the studio. When I asked him about Jeanne and reminded him of the bees, he looked at me with his pale blue eyes smiling nostalgically, and said, '*Ah, l'élan révolutionnaire de la jeunesse!*' It was strange to realize that I was now part of his nostalgia.

Michel is a small man, easily recognizable from his photographs, but older-looking. His movements are all a kind of dance, but he has sad, charming eyes, whilst the combination of his long curly hair and his perfectly cut suit lends him the distinction of unconventional success. And what perhaps most makes his success unconventional is the fact that he has remained benign, disarming.

When Janos opened the studio door, Michel flung his arms round him, greeting him in French. Then he stepped back and looked at Janos.

'*You haven't changed a bit. Not one bit,*' *he said in English, adding as an odd-sounding colloquialism* '*Dear Bloke.*' '*But I am fatter. No?*' *And he patted his stomach as he might have patted a child's head.*

He kissed Diana's hand whilst she was still suspicious of him, and greeted Hancock who, as always when he first meets a stranger, stood awkwardly to attention like a new conscript. Mrs Hancock, however, rose to the occasion, and he lingered over her fingers. She is a remarkably competent woman. Given a Paris dressmaker, she could take the place of Michel's mistress at any Paris vernissage.

After the greetings Michel stood in the centre of the studio and looked round.

'*Marvellous, marvellous, mon vieux.*'

He stared at The Games, *put his forefinger and thumb together in a gesture for denoting perfection, kissed the air with his lips and taking Janos's arm, said:*

'Formidable! *Beautiful!*'

At dinner he bought bottle after bottle of wine for us. After a few glasses, Hancock lost his shyness.

'*You're really a painter in Paris?*' *he inquired.*

Michel said he had lived there all his life, and Hancock shook his head in envious admiration.

'*Do you hear that, Vee?*'

'*You find that romantic?*' *asked Michel.*

'*Of course.*' *Hancock fiddled with the spectacles on his nose.* '*It's the capital of art and wine and love. Isn't it?*'

Michel raised his glass. '*To the capital of wine!*'

But despite the slight irony of this toast, it was obvious that Michel was delighted, and when later he discovered that Hancock was a butcher by profession, he was even more delighted. He had always wanted to design a ballet round a butcher's shop, he said, the mademoiselle shoppers dancing with the pigs, and the butcher with his striped apron as a kind of procuress. Then he turned to Janos, and asked him in a whisper what Hancock's paintings were like – were they Primitive?

It was hard to say whether Michel or Hancock was the more naïve. Yet even Diana finally succumbed to Michel's charm. He was sure, he told her, that she was a writer. She had a writer's face. She worked in a library. Eh bien, to Literature!

Janos asked him how his exhibition was going. Very well. He had sold about a third on the first day. When was Janos's next exhibition to be? Janos laughed – like a professional to an amateur's question.

'I do not exhibit,' he said.

'Ah! You do not find it necessary. Your collectors come to the studio?'

'Ask this man here,' Janos said.

I described to him the London set-up and Janos's position. Whilst I spoke, Michel nodded sympathetically, but when I had finished, he insisted:

'Mais non! C'est incroyable. Incroyable.' Then he turned to Janos. 'You should have stayed in Paris.'

'The capital of art,' put in Hancock.

A few days later both Janos and I went to see Michel's show at the Malvern Galleries. The paintings were brightly coloured, decorative, poetic: their subjects – butterflies, fishes, lovers, hybrid birds, fantastic flowers. A few had something of the old surrealistic, sinister shock-value, but the majority were dreamy, formalized and lyrical. The skill behind them was considerable. But they were slight and although highly sophisticated, whimsical. A large canvas dominated one of the galleries. It was called La Machine à fleurs, and represented a kind of mill-wheel of flowers, turning on a spindle which was a woman. Beside the wheel was a red dog, barking.

Michel came into the gallery. As he did so, he glanced at his paintings as a hurrying celebrity glances at the small crowd that has

*gathered. He embraced Janos, and said how much he had enjoyed
the other night. So had we.*

*'And the butcher-painter's wife, she is very beautiful,' Michel
added.*

'Very,' said Janos.

*We looked away towards the pictures on the walls. Janos said
nothing. I asked the old stop-gap question: Were they all recent
works? And so we began to talk without expressing any opinion.
But eventually Michel asked Janos outright what he thought of* La
Machine à fleurs. *Janos, tall and gaunt in his overcoat, stared
severely at the painting.*

'I do not understand it,' he said at last.

'I do not understand it altogether myself,' replied Michel.

'And the title? Did you think of that afterwards?'

'Of course.'

'Then what did you want this to mean?'

Michel went up to Janos and took his arm.

*'Mon dieu! You are the same as ever. The same Jansenist mind.
You're a formidably strict man, Janos. You haven't changed a bit.'
He laughed and looked back at his own canvas as though to find his
explanation. 'I suppose what I meant to suggest was the – how shall
I say it? – the ruthlessness, you feel? – of romantic love. The woman
turns round as on an iron – what is the word? – the iron one uses
for cooking a piece of meat, as also in the Inquisition, and the
flowers, the garlands, they go round her to make her pretty but to
change nothing.'*

'And the dog?'

*'The dog is the animal. The little dog is not deceived by the
flowers. He just barks at her sex. And I call it* La Machine à fleurs
*because the machine has no conscience. The machine, she is remorse-
less.'*

*Michel watched Janos continue to stare silently at the painting.
At last Janos spoke in his loud, broken voice.*

*'Not many days ago I watched a man who was a mechanic.
Perhaps half an hour I watched him without a word. He was
putting together the wheels of a gear. Very patient, very gentle,
as you say – like a botanist who loves the flowers. It is a lonely job,
I say to him. And he agreed, and said real mechanics they are
boring people because they are always inside their machines. In*

your precision-tool shop, he said, your mates are not very sociable. It is not like drivers or steel men. It is a special gift? I asked him. Gift! he said, I suppose so, but not many times I do a job as I want to. There's always the customer's pocket and you have to do the job too quickly. He was a shy man, but now I had made him talk. All these engines you see, he said, all these engines, sometimes I get dead scared of them. The young boys don't know enough; if they did they wouldn't begin. When I am hearing an engine running, I can see every part moving. I can see every part. And supposing I hear a bad noise. One bearing is worn. I see in my mind, immediate, what is wrong. Then I see this wrong go from part to part, from one to the other, like a dirty piece of gossip, he said. And I get dead scared, he said, unless I can do the job as I want to. This mechanic man, who can judge by instinct to two thou, as he calls it – he is the only conscience of the machine I understand. A fine two-thou conscience.' Janos pronounced thou as tou – and at first I did not understand what he meant. Michel, I'm sure, never did. 'And so I ask you how is it you believe the machine remorseless? My mechanic said he was scared. But it was not because of the machine, but because he might not do the job as well as he wished.'

Michel laughed, but was puzzled – as well he might have been. At last he said:

'You wish I had painted a painting of a machine through the eyes of your mechanic?'

'Not at all,' replied Janos, rubbing his temple with one hand and looking towards the door. 'Not at all.'

Michel laughed again because there was nothing else to say, and we all moved away from the painting.

Later Michel brought a book over to us, and said, 'There's a photograph of you here.'

The photograph, taken in the thirties, showed Janos, Michel and another man in a Paris studio. It was a good studio snapshot – including cigarette-stubs, the drawings pinned to the wall and that air of an urgent conversation – almost a plot – having been interrupted. Janos, in an open-necked shirt, looked thinner and more determined but less severe. Michel, beaming, had one hand on Janos's shoulder and looked like a genial café patron.

Janos turned the pages. The book was called Portrait of Michel C. ... *At the back were recent photographs: Michel with his*

159

grandchildren; Michel in evening dress at the theatre; Michel
talking to a film-star; Michel in a rose garden.
   Janos handed the book back with a smile.
   'A long time ago,' he said. 'Much has happened.'
   Michel looked uncomfortable.
   'Mais tu sais – you're exactly the same Jansci, exactly!'
   My own guess is that it was from that moment that Michel
decided to try to persuade the gallery, his gallery, to give Janos an
exhibition.

NOVEMBER 15

No one really knows how we work. When I think back on my
early work, I see the regular repetition of various ideas of which
I was quite unaware at the time. Now I suddenly realize that my
two anonymous heads against the night could conceivably be
Laszlo and myself twenty years ago. Not likenesses, but enough
to shake me when I realized it. Twenty years ago. I can count on
ten more for working. Twenty if very lucky.

NOVEMBER 17

Michel considers my life to be tragic. I can see this in the way he
reassures me – in order perhaps to reassure himself. I suppose
many others might agree with him. Yet it is not and has not
been tragic. My work bears witness to that. A narrative of it all
might make it seem so. That, however, is the kind of distortion
which is inevitable to the narrative. It has to leave out of account
all the stray, uneventful moments – just as a map leaves out of
account millions of flowers. It is in these moments that one
recovers; delights in the fact that one has survived so far and is
critically aware without a crisis. Also, I have worked. It is
tempting to turn the tables and say Michel's life is tragic. But to
do that would only be to seek indirect consolation for myself.
It is not true. He is a happy man. Our ways are simply different.
He was born less discontented than I.

NOVEMBER 26

Have begun a canvas of a welder. I watch him in the workshop
round the corner. Despite gloves and mask, his action must have
the precision of a Renaissance Cupid touching Venus's tit. But

160

calm. Calm. We must find our forms as a wide river settles for its course across a flat plain. In the back of my mind is a childhood memory of a flame-eater at the winter fair: a desperate-looking man, hungry-looking, but with his cheeks blown out as if with water and a great stream of flame gushing out of his mouth and lighting up his dilated nostrils, his half-closed eyes and the faces of the crowd, with a terrible chiaroscuro, the chiaroscuro of superstition such as you find in the late Goyas. The difference between that terrible superstitious flame turning a man's mouth into the entrance to a medieval hell, between that and the flame of a welder, used in the most precise way that heat has ever been used by man – that is the difference, the advance that I struggle towards with my classicism. Maybe it is also the difference between Hungary yesterday and today. Another reason why I should be there.

DECEMBER 3

The Malvern Gallery has phoned up and asked if they might come to see my work. Obviously Michel is behind it. I have not told Diana in case it falls through. The light on the river tonight was superb: the water – neon viridian.

DECEMBER 7

Waiting for the visit of the gallery disturbs my working. Like royalty in a coal-mine. I cannot decide what to show them. Diana looks suspiciously at my burrowing about behind the old piles.

DECEMBER 12

They have been. An old fat man and a thin young one. The fat man looked like an official eunuch inspecting a harem; the young one looked too tired to respond in any way – he had had his pleasures hours ago. I sat them in chairs side by side and lifted, one after another, about thirty paintings on to the easel for them to inspect. Fortunately, the light was quite good. I showed them paintings from the last ten years – from three and a half thousand working days in this secluded studio. I am not a great innovator – none of my generation has been. But the best of us have fixed a way of painting, a way of looking at the world which cannot now be gone back upon. Have you anything smaller? said the fat man. My answer was to uncover *The Games*. This really frightened them. We couldn't possibly get that into the gallery, said the young man. Then the old man spoke. He said that my work was most interesting and made a lot of English work seem – here he was at a loss for words. Could he bring another partner along tomorrow? Tomorrow, I said, I shall be out. The next day then? That depends on how good the light is, I said. It is no good your coming here in a fog. I will phone you. The young man left his yellow kid gloves behind.

1956

JANUARY 22
I am to have an exhibition. Twenty-five paintings next October.

The reader may deduce from this that Michel must have argued very persuasively. Michel's charm is very persuasive. But I doubt whether this was the deciding factor. Picture-dealing when concerned with comparatively unknown artists is always a gamble; sometimes a whole show sells out; sometimes not a single work is bought. Consequently a kind of superstition, a kind of magic of success, holds some sway over the decisions of even the hard-boiled. Michel was highly successful; therefore his tips might be so, too. Or, if the directors of the Malvern Gallery did calculate, they probably calculated that it was worth pleasing Michel by giving his friend a show, even if it flopped. I insist that the decision had nothing to do with Janos's paintings as such, for the simple reason that the same gallery had unequivocally rejected examples of his work a few months before. The other fact which may have influenced them was Janos's own behaviour. He behaved awkwardly and rudely. He insisted upon having a photograph of The Games *included in the show. He insisted upon not having frames round his canvases. He asked unusually high prices. He refused to supply them with biographical notes. And all this – much as it would have horrified Janos to know it – undoubtedly impressed them. 'No, Madam, I think we ought to approach the artist on your behalf. He is rather difficult, you understand?'*

Diana wept this evening with excitement. I tried to warn her that an exhibition doesn't necessarily promise much in itself.

Despite his cautiousness, Janos was nevertheless pleased by the prospect of the exhibition. He gave a party to celebrate the news and now, looking back on it, I cannot remember many other occasions when both he and Diana were so carefree. Not that they did anything special, it was simply a question of atmosphere. Max came to the party – there were about twenty people altogether – and for once there was no quarrel. The Hancocks took the news as a matter of course. They firmly believe that the best artists are not fully appreciated until they are dead, and this was just the beginning of the process. George and June Trent were appeased but still indignant. 'About time, too,' said George. 'Look at the muck they hang most of the time.' A number of students from the art school were also there, and two girls in black jeans and their hair in pony-tails distributed the glasses of mulled wine that Janos, looking rather like a wizard, served from a huge brass bowl on top of the stove. Several of George's young painter friends peeped surreptitiously behind canvases that had their backs towards them. The athletes in The Games *towered above us. The reds and blacks in the painting were brighter and sharper than any colours among the crowd. It is a painting that needs people around it. Diana put on some records, and we began to dance. When we were a little tight, Max made us all roar with laughter by his imitation of various dancing techniques. A couple of students lay whispering together on the divan. Diana performed a Scottish reel. It was a normal enough studio party, but happy. Undoubtedly happy.*

FEBRUARY 6

Looking through my folio of etchings, I have decided that I should also try to exhibit these. Some of the old plates can still stand another ten or so prints being pulled. Printed most of the day. Etching is the best medium for working at in the cold weather.

FEBRUARY 18

It snowed last night. Today colours were themselves again in the reflected light. Unfortunately I had to teach.

163

Worked all day on *The Welder*.

Stalin is accused of a cult of personality. His portraits are now being removed. They were terrible paintings. But I do not like the phrase. A man need not be attacked because he is great. The real question is the meaning of Equality. There are good economic reasons why economic equality cannot be established during one revolutionary night. But the concept need not be dropped. And it need not become hypocritical. In the name of freedom – even the first freedom: the freedom not to starve – there is a voluptuousness. Delacroix was right there. But in the name of equality there is in the same way a moral severity that Lenin expressed right down to his choice of the boots he wore. Fraternity, when we have it, will resolve the differences between Delacroix' goddess of the Greeks and Lenin's humble, strong, practical boots. But in the meanwhile, remember how equality is severe. It does not deny individual prestige, but it refuses palace walls, luxury, pomp. But I am a painter. I have never had the opportunity to live in any other way. And, surprisingly, most artists have austere tastes. . . . It may not be important.

FEBRUARY 23

The snow has turned to slush. I spent the afternoon in the greyness working on *The Welder* again. Every winter there were always a few nights when the wind and frost were right. In the morning I woke to see every twig of every tree, every blade of grass, with a razor of ice on its leeward side. Sometimes this ice would be three inches deep on a twig thinner than string. In the sunlight this white-frosted ice would pinken enough to look like blossom. But it is the pine trees that are most beautiful. The trees of the Bakony Forest. On these the wind whips the ice round the needles till every bough hangs low with the weight, and the ice forms itself round the needles in the shape of feathers, silver feathers shot like silk with light. Each bough becomes the outstretched wing of a giant crystal bird. These sights were my fairy stories.

MARCH 10

Gough told me this joke at the school today. After Gide had died he sent a telegram to Claudel saying, Look Out! *L'enfer n'existe pas.*

MARCH 19
LASZLO WAS INNOCENT. *Laci te gyere idea.*

'*Laci come here*' – *a line from a poem by Petöfi.*

APRIL 1

I have nothing to write. He *was* married. I would like to see his wife. Words lie. My brush does not. All around people are talking. But I have nothing to say. I have begun a canvas of some roses.

APRIL

If only there was a gentle god. For the first thirty seconds when I wake in the morning I am free.

APRIL

There is a woman living with me whose name is Diana.

GOD KNOWS THE DATE

The roses are finished. I painted them for Laszlo's rehabilitation.

MAY DAY

In the summer the horses lay down on the Puszta, and from a distance the mounds of their bellies on the side of the earth made them look like carcasses. You thought they were dead. But when you got near them they stood up on their long legs and trotted away from you. That was an easy reprieve. You, my one-time comrade, will lie for ever on the side of the earth.

MAY 6

What have I believed? And what I disbelieved? Can I work my way back?

MAY 7

To my credit	*Debit*
200 paintings	Desertion
A few etchings	Disloyalty
Still being alive	Dependence

JUNE 11

If I had painted still-lives and clouds, I might have continued indefinitely.

JUNE 14

Like all exiles eventually, I have become academic. My studio has become my own museum.

JULY 12

I have filled a book of drawings of women at love. I have done no more for weeks. Katinka yawning: minutes later the muscles of her throat taut like ropes for coming like a song. Blaise – why was she always known by a man's name? – white with hair the colour of gladioli. Elsa like a dark violin. Simone who always wept on my chest and tore my back with her nails. My pig because she slept as content as a pig. My cony because she jumped like one. Rosie in English fields. Thus I reconstruct my innocence.

JULY 24

It is in dreams that we often first discover real and actual possibilities of freedom.

JULY 27

A question for the West:
Have the executioners of Sacco and Vanzetti ever proclaimed their victim's innocence?
A question for myself:
Did the comrades of Sacco and Vanzetti ever believe in their guilt?

AUGUST 4

It is I who have been left behind. Laszlo is gone and his comrades, guilty and innocent, have advanced. Some by their own deaths and others by investigation and admission, they have gone beyond what has happened. It cannot happen again. It is I who have been left behind – I who never declared his innocence even to myself. Because he would not have understood my work? Because he would not have understood my work? For that?

166

AUGUST 10

I must pilot all anguish to port. Only then can I be useful.

SEPTEMBER 5

For the first time for twenty years I do not paint. I only use my eyes. I stand and watch the fruit markets. The flower stalls in London are the only things that remind me what colour can be. I walk miles every day. Suddenly London has again become a foreign city to me. But I cannot paint and I have to force myself to say much to my students. I must wait. I walk around every day like a man who finds, on a fine afternoon in a foreign city, that he has hours to wait for his train, and so uses this unexpected time to explore a place that otherwise he might never have seen. I have been to Dulwich, the Isle of Dogs, Hampton Court, Islington, Bow. I have walked down hundreds of streets that were unfamiliar to me. Occasionally I think that I have seen the same child twice. Possibly they will now name a short street after Laszlo. When London becomes a Socialist capital, it will happen without a single street name being changed. In that lies the foreignness of England.

When I read these last entries I can scarcely believe that they were written by the man I saw once or twice every week during the summer and early autumn of 1956. It is true that Janos was not working much at that time. I remember noticing this and putting it down to anxiety about his exhibition. It is also true that he looked tired and strained, as he periodically did. It is true, too, that he was somewhat silent. But from none of this would it have been conceivable even to suspect that he was suffering this most acute anguish. Such self-control was not, I think, practised as a virtue. Looking back, I am now certain that he simply thought that it was impossible to hope that any of his intimates could understand the crisis he was facing. And in this I think he was right.

SEPTEMBER 28

There is much we do not know. Come to terms with it. Fear of the unknown has been exploited to impose tyranny after tyranny upon man in the name of hell-fire. Hell was always more effective than Heaven as an ideological weapon. It was Heaven the heretics took over. No need to fall in love with the unknown – that way lies every kind of superstition and all the products of the Dream Factory. But no need to despise it either. That way lies the bureaucracy that comes between men in the form of a door with a guard posted outside day and night. Respect for the unknown. Then inevitably respect for the conscience. In face of the unknown, one can only rely on conscience. The mind needs knowledge. The heart needs interest. I begin to find my conscience. I must test it.

OCTOBER 2

The exhibition opens in a week's time. The protestation of innocence.

This is what happened on the afternoon of the private view. We left the studio at about three. Janos had his best suit on and a white shirt. As always, his smart clothes emphasized how much like an unpeeled potato his face was. Smart clothes demand perfectly boiled potatoes. In the same way his white cuffs could not but emphasize the printers' ink ingrained into his hands.

Diana wore a hat with a bent feather which encircled one side of her face and almost tickled her chin. Yet, to do her justice, she looked superb. She betrayed her nervousness only very occasionally, and then just by turning over the gloves she carried in her hand. Otherwise she created for herself single-handed the kind of dignity that the occasion creates for a bride at a wedding or a widow at a funeral. It was impossible to see her – or, anyway, to see her and know her – and not to be moved. Until this moment she had made nothing but sacrifices for Janos, and now she was convinced that today was to be the turning point of justice, the beginning of the period of rewards.

She got out of the taxi and entered the gallery, not as if she owned it (Diana was incapable of any kind of flamboyance), but as if she were certain she was being anxiously awaited. She had been to the gallery several times to check arrangements – Janos always procrastinated about going, and had formed an alliance with the first partner by which it was understood that for all social and administrative affairs Janos should be by-passed as much as possible. It was a little as if it were a posthumous exhibition, and Diana the painter's widow.

As for the actual and living Janos, left to pay the taxi-driver, he was morose and silent. But then so are many painters at the prospect of their own private view.

Inside, the young partner came up to us. (He is the son of the third partner.) He took us into the first gallery where Janos's paintings were hung. I had seen them before, but Janos had not. He looked round the walls suspiciously and quickly, as if checking whether a canvas had been stolen. None had.

'It looks very well, don't you think?' said the young man.

Janos said nothing, but went up to examine the canvas of The Waves *to see if it had been scratched.*

'You've hung them beautifully,' said Diana.

The Malvern Gallery always runs two exhibitions concurrently. Janos's fellow exhibitor was H——, one of England's leading abstract painters. Through the entrance to the second gallery we could now see H—— being photographed in front of one of his pictures. The photographer had obviously suggested that he should take off his coat and roll his sleeves up, for he stood there, pipe in his mouth and bare arms folded – as if posing for a study of the Gentleman Farmer at Home. Diana immediately looked towards Janos to see how he would photograph. He still had on his large dark ancient military-looking overcoat and his best beret. But her plans were at least temporarily foiled because Janos insisted that there was no point in hanging about and that we should go and have some coffee. She did not argue with him. Today he would be coaxed.

After a while H—— came into the same coffee-house and, seeing us, walked over. He is a man of about Janos's age with an unworried, apple-like face and bushy brown eyebrows. He wore a very pale grey suit, a blue shirt with white stripes and a tangerine tie.

'May I introduce myself? I'm H——. You're Lavin, aren't you?' He pulled back a chair and sat down with us.

'We've got a fine day at least,' he said.

Janos looked at him.

'Do you think the weather makes so much difference?' asked Diana.

'To tell the truth, I've no idea. All I know is I hate private views – when they're my own. But they're even worse in the States where I've just had a show. They really crawl all over you there. Like pink elephants. And the journalists! All the time they're

169

asking you questions. "Now, tell us, Mr. H— ," he imitated an American voice, "do you figure abstract art is going to be the one and only of the future ?" As if I should know!'

He shrugged his shoulders at the memory. His eyes were pale blue and constantly amused. Although he must work far harder than the theory justifies, he believes that Art is essentially Play. His coffee arrived and he brought out of his hip-pocket a pigskin-and-chromium flask with brandy in it.

'Let me lace your drinks,' he said with the trace of an American manner outlasting his imitation.

'Thank you,' said Janos.

'Every winter breakfast-time my father used to have cognac with his coffee,' said Diana. 'I haven't seen anyone else drink it for years.'

'Did you ever meet Feininger in the United States?' asked Janos.

"'Fraid not. He's certainly made some very, very pretty things.' Janos retired back to his coffee-cup.

'So the brandy brings back childhood memories, Mrs Lavin?'

The conversation continued like this for a few minutes until suddenly H— heard a newspaper seller shouting outside. He glanced at his watch, shouted, 'Back in a tick,' and rushed out. When he returned he was beaming all over his face – even his eyebrows somehow smiling.

'I got the winner of the two-thirty. Sixteen to one. Well. That was certainly a long shot. But it's a good beginning for the day, isn't it?'

Diana laughed with him. And we went back to the gallery.

People were beginning to arrive. As soon as we entered, the third partner seized hold of Janos's arm with one hand and Diana's with the other. He is fairish, going bald, with small eyes and a thin inturned mouth that suggests he is constantly smoking a pipe, although I have never seen him with one.

'I don't know whether my son mentioned it to you, but we've had the buyer for the Holland Bequest round here several times, and he is very interested in The Waves. Just now he asked us to reserve it – for Montreal.' He smiled at them both in turn, closed his lips and sucked. Then he released Janos's arm, but continued leading Diana into the crowd. Janos raised one eyebrow at me. After that I lost sight of him, and all I can describe now is what I saw myself.

I was surprised by the number of people. The gallery, once they had agreed to Janos's exhibition, must have called up all the support and interest they could for 'an unknown but very interesting Hungarian painter'. Sharing the galleries with H— was also a considerable advantage. H— automatically guaranteed a large number of people, yet because his paintings are all very much the same, a whole roomful of them, however much you may admire their purity, becomes a little boring; consequently, many of his guests drifted, I think, into Janos's room.

Many of the faces I knew without being able to put a name to them. One sees them regularly at all the best art functions. Suddenly, emerging from these familiar unknowns there appeared Marcus Aurelius. He leered at me and put a heavy hand round the back of the neck of the girl at his side.

'I don't think you know Jeannie,' he said.

Jeannie, who looked as though she had only just been tugged out of bed and wanted only to be back there with Marcus, said in a slow sleepy voice:

'You really admire this man, do you?'

'Yes, I do.'

'I wish I could be with you,' she said so gently that at first I thought she was whispering her longing to Marcus, 'I wish I could be with you. But I just can't see it.'

'And you?' I nodded at Marcus.

'I perfectly see why Jeannie doesn't like it. It's very unfeminine. Almost entirely cerebral. Without any appeal to the senses.' As he said 'senses' he opened one of his hands expressively to demonstrate all that the paintings lacked: his finger-nails were badly bitten. 'At the same time,' he continued, 'I admit that in their way they are impressive. Rather in the same way, I should have thought, as Puvis de Chavannes.'

He put his hand over Jeannie's shoulder and spoke with all the pleasant self-consciousness of a man being watched by a pair of hypnotized eyes. 'Do you know the story about Ingres taking his students round the Louvre? When they passed the Delacroix, he used to say – "Messieurs, levez vos chapeaux mais ne regardez pas."

'That's rather what I feel about this work. You know, the return to Classicism, the restraint, the Poussinesque unity – we can

only applaud. But let's face it too – it's terribly, monumentally boring.'

'Shhh!' said Jeannie, pushing her lips out into a bunch, 'he may be able to hear you, darling.'

I looked round. Janos was invisible. I could only catch a glimpse of Diana talking to one of her friends – a pair of black and a pair of white gloves playing Touch together.

Marcus had also looked round and now bent down to his girl. 'I won't be a minute, cherry-pie. There's someone over there I must just have a word with.'

In the entrance to H — 's room stood the curator of the leading public gallery of the country. Marcus stood near him whilst he talked to N — .

I left Jeannie to the mercy of her man's ambitions and drifted away. Occasionally I heard Marcus laughing loudly at, I suppose, one of the curator's sallies. Most of the time, however, it was impossible to distinguish any single voice unless the speaker was at one's elbow. The room was filled with the rackety engine noise of cocktail-party conversation, and indeed waiters were now squeezing their way through the crowd distributing glasses of sherry. It was impossible to see any of the large paintings properly. The few visitors who were conscientiously looking at the pictures had to stand right in front of them, like people in the front row pressed against the railings along a race-track. A man lit a cigar, and a woman beside him in a turquoise hat took down an address in her diary. Between them I saw the simplified head of one of The Swimmers.

Looking vaguely for Janos, I ran into Diana. To say that she was beside herself gives the wrong impression. She was, but she was also in complete control. No longer as solemn as a bride, she was now more like a girl of the nineteenth century at her engagement ball, whose heart is constantly fluttering with excitement but who suspects that the whole room is watching her.

'John,' she exclaimed, 'look!' Then, clearing a way through the crowd effortlessly because with complete proprietary confidence, she led me to the canvas of The Welder. *A red star was stuck to the thin strip of wood that surrounded it instead of a frame.*

'My brother-in-law has just bought it,' she whispered.

I smiled, said something appropriate and looked at her. Did she

*realize that a family sale would be somewhat suspect to Janos?
Probably. The wedding, the honeymoon, the marriage all lay ahead;
this was only the beginning.*

There was a commotion at the front door of the gallery.

*''Course I've lost my card. Still, I'm invited. Invited, I say. Go
and ask the artists. Thank you. Thank you.'*

*The door-keeper let the man in – a man of about forty-five in
untidy clothes – to avoid a scene. He did not appear to be very
drunk, and he was obviously not a gate-crasher because several
people, looking up at the disturbance, had waved to him.*

*He walked happily down into the first gallery – a passenger
going aboard a ship. His face was flushed, and the very coarse
texture of the pores of his skin made it look even more like a not
quite ripe strawberry. Yet it is an attractive face because of its almost constant expression of happy, tolerant perplexity. Harry is well
known in journalist and literary circles. Janos had known him
during the war and, indeed, it had been through him that Janos's
book of drawings had been published. In the thirties he fought in
Spain and wrote a good novel about the Middle East. Now, when
he has the money, he haunts the Bohemian drinking clubs and is
usually tight. He hates two things passionately: the class system and
Communist Party edicts about art. This is somewhat reasonable
because it is these two things that have destroyed him.*

'Where's Janos?' he demanded loudly.

*Diana, for one moment whilst she decided what to do, showed her
displeasure. Then she advanced towards him.*

'Harry, how nice of you to come. Janos is along there.'

*She pushed him into the crowd and turned to me. 'Do try to find
him,' she said, 'he's disappeared.'*

*I made my way round the gallery. Jeannie, still deserted by
Marcus, was now talking to a young man with jeans like her own
and a crew-cut.*

*'The paint must be felt,' she was saying. 'You must want to
touch it like a fruit or a horse or' – she hesitated for a second to give
emphasis to the alternative – 'or a body.'*

*I pushed on, but was stopped by the director of one of our national
art organizations. Behind me two women were talking.*

'What a gorgeous ring!'

'It's Roman.'

'*I guessed so. Before Christ surely?*'

The national art organizer peered down at me through the glasses on his nose and through the glass of sherry held up to his mouth.

'*How is it we've never seen this man's work before?*' *he inquired.*

'*He's never shown before.*'

He finished the rest of his sherry.

'*What do you think of his work, then?*' *I asked.*

'*Some yes, some no.*'

'*Yes.*'

'*Some I find too cold.*'

'*The nudes?*'

'*No, I like the nudes.*'

'*What else do you like?*'

'*The one over there. What does he call it, now?*' *He looked through his bifocal lenses at the catalogue. '*Yes, The Waves. That seems to me to be a very remarkable achievement. Perhaps trying to do what Monet did – the later Monet, of course – but starting from the opposite direction, if you follow me! One could, of course, enumerate the influences, couldn't one? A little Villon, a little Léger, a little de la Fresnaye, perhaps?*' *Nearly all his sentences ended on a note of interrogation. He studied his catalogue again. The ticks or crosses that this man writes against works in catalogues carry considerable weight. Frequently they make all the difference between a work being bought or not bought by the public art organizations.*

'*There are quite a few others,*' *he continued, '*that I think are* horrid.*' *He gave the childish word official prestige.*

'*How do you mean, horrid?*'

*He smiled. A cautious smile. He is a man who does not like committing himself with arguments, because it may always be necessary to change them. To commit oneself to an opinion is different, because this can always be overruled even – generously – by oneself, as having been '*purely personal*'. '*Rhetorical,*' *he modified.* '*Inflated, perhaps?*'

A young girl came to his side.

'*Have you met my daughter Jennifer?*'

'*Daddy, can I have some sherry?*' *He looked round about him for an example.*

'I don't see why not,' he said.

'I think these paintings are terribly good,' Jennifer went on with all the emphatic conviction that seventeen-year-olds can have in their own discoveries. 'Don't you, Daddy? Much, much more exciting than old Henry H —'s things. Even if Henry is a family friend. They're beautiful, specially the ones with the huge figures and looking like statues. I adore them.'

'You see,' her father turned to me, his cautious smile troubling his mouth, 'I think them rhetorical. She thinks them wonderful. Perhaps it's just a question of generation? Of what we're brought up on?'

He shrugged his shoulders and, leaving the question in the air, he moved, tall and stooping, towards a waiter to change his empty glass for a full one.

'You're not as old fashioned as all that, Daddy,' I heard his daughter saying.

I looked round further for Janos. He was clearly not in the gallery. Perhaps he was in H— 's room. I paused because two voices behind me were discussing The Swimmers.

'Do you know what it reminds me of?' asked a woman's voice. 'Those turtles in the aquarium.'

'By the way,' replied a man's voice, 'I meant to ask you. A chap offered me shares in a turtle today. Five quid. Would you like some to make soup with?'

'Lovely, Hugo. Yum, yum.'

The prospect in H—'s gallery was the same as in Janos's and it was equally crowded. The only difference was that H— himself was visible as a centre of interest. There were two rows of people round him instead of the ordinary conversational one. Since he is a short man, one couldn't actually see his face; but I glimpsed the flash of his tangerine tie against the blue shirt. Marcus was dissertating at length about one of H—'s paintings to the gallery curator, who was a much smaller man than Marcus, and so was, as it were, both embraced and trapped by Marcus's sweeping gestures and manual demonstrations. The curator's wife stood near by, as deserted as Jeannie, because, for opposite reasons, her man also had to keep in touch; Marcus might one day be a useful ally for keeping a sharper man than Marcus out.

Voices came from several directions.

'All these new plays about the Resistance. What I say is that it's time we organized a resistance against the Resistance!'

'I couldn't agree more. It's all hate, hate, hate, nowadays. And it's so silly. After all, we've all suffered, haven't we?'

'And then there was a delightful invention. A bed which as you vibrated on the mattress, dear, had little Eastern fans to fan you. And in every room there was a different sort of bed with a different sort of girl. Even a broken-down bed in a working-class kitchen. And they said all the sons of the aristocracy chose that one. Such a pity they banned it. They should at least have turned it into a museum. It was quite unique, with quite quite delightful paintings on the wardrobes.'

There was no sign of Janos.

I went downstairs to look in the lavatory. The noise of the crowd in the two rooms upstairs sounded weird from down there in the basement. There was much more stamping and thumping than one would have expected. It sounded as though some machine were being rather irregularly driven, the fairly constant noise of the voices being the purr of the engine itself. I walked between racks with hundreds of paintings on them. A few were recognizable even from the few inches at one side that one could see as one passed – Utrillo, Modigliani, Soutine. (All men who lead such desperate lives that their bad paintings are easy to fake.) I tried the lavatory door. It was locked. I tried the handle again.

'Is that you, Janos?' came Harry's thick voice. 'Hang on. I've got a wonderful story to tell you –'

So Janos wasn't there. I went upstairs again into the engine-rooms.

Diana saw me. I have compared her to a bride and a fiancée. Now, almost entranced, she was like a believer cured at a holy shrine. I looked hard at her. Her hat was still in perfect position. The galleries were by now stifling, but her face was perfectly powdered. Only her eyes were possessed. She took my arm and said quietly:

'We've sold two more. Do find him.'

'Who to?'

'That man over there – he's a Hungarian jeweller, and a woman somewhere else. Perhaps he's gone to have another cup of coffee. Do try to find him.'

'*I'll go and see.*'

I was surprised that she was not more worried or anyway annoyed by Janos's absence. But presumably she had expected him to duck out if he could. Her terms of partnership were not in their own way so unreasonable: he should paint the pictures and she would arrange the rest.

The third partner was standing by the door with his son. The son leant against the wall, played with the change in his pocket and was clearly bored: another whole hour to go. The father had built up the business – the Malvern Gallery is one of the richest in London, and for him the old excitement of pitting his eye against other dealers (his eye for three separate categories of art: for what the public wants now; for what it will want the year after next; and for what it will rave about in twenty years' time) could still be thrilling.

'*Sir Gerald Banks has just arrived,*' *he pointed to a car out-side.*

'*Did many critics come this morning?*' *I asked. His eyes were fixed on the car.*

'*Quite a few,*' *he said without turning round.* '*We'll see. We'll see when the papers come out.*'

The car door opened and he advanced to open the door of the gallery. The son remained staring at the toes of his shoes.

I slipped out with a hurried wave of the hand and went round to the coffee-bar. It was fairly full, but Janos was not there. I went up to the girl behind the counter.

'*Do you remember four of us having coffee here about an hour and a half ago?*'

'*I wasn't on then.*'

'*Oh, well, has a tall man with a long dark overcoat and a beret been in here?*'

'*With a red beard?*'

'*No, without a beard. A thin kind of face with screwed-up eyes and a foreign accent.*'

'*We get lots like that.*'

'*I think you'd remember him.*'

'*Well, I can't say I can.*'

Probably he hadn't been here. I sighed. Then the girl leant forward.

'He told me to tell anyone who was looking for him he'd be back before the show was over.'

'Is that all?'

'That's all. He was very charming. He looked just like one of those spies you read about.'

I was furious. I could understand his escaping from the gallery for a while, but this kind of plotting and message-leaving was childish. Perhaps I was also somewhat disturbed; it sounded so unlike Janos. Outside in the street, I turned in the opposite direction to the gallery and walked on, trying to work out what I should do next. I only got angrier. Outside a news cinema I turned round, having decided to go back. I glanced at the photographs of what was showing. And there, coming out of the cinema, was Janos.

'What the hell are you doing? Everyone's looking for you.'

'I was taking a little relief.'

'Why do you leave messages with waitresses in coffee-bars?'

'Messages? What messages?'

He looked puzzled – more, I think, at my anger than at the question. He put his hand on my shoulder.

'What is the matter?' he asked. 'You take it all too seriously. There are only certain situations in which you can be serious. If you want to be serious, you must choose them.'

You have a knack for turning an argument, I thought.

'Did you or did you not leave a message with the waitress in the coffee-bar?'

'I demand you, would I? Of course not.'

We went on in silence. Janos, coat open, walked with his long, dog-like strides. It was a blind kind of walk that tended to make other people step out of his way. After a moment, he added:

'I stuck it for one hour. I came out for half an hour. Now we are going back. What is the matter?'

'You have sold three paintings.'

'Good. I am very glad. Diana must be happy.'

When we got to the door of the gallery, he stopped and stared at me intensely. Round his eyes were dark brown shadows. The potato looked dirtier than ever.

'Judge people as you have known them. Do not jump to conclusions. It took me a long time to learn.'

'All right. All right.' I said.

'If I don't sell the big nude – would you like it?'

'I'd love it.'

He slapped my face affectionately and entered the gallery. I was to have reason not to forget his words.

Inside, Janos's room seemed a little emptier. There were also more people whom I recognized. Max and the Hancocks had arrived. The impression that the room was emptier may, however, have only been the result of the presence of Sir Gerald Banks, for Banks cleared a space around himself. No rule was observed; sometimes a person or a couple stepped into the space. Nor was it, I think, the result of anything deliberate on his part. Simply, a man of commanding size and posture with that kind of nonchalance that is the unique mark of great wealth, entered the room, and although not averse to exchanging words with those whom he knew, clearly wanted to study the paintings – this somehow penetrated the consciousness of those who were drinking, talking, manoeuvring, hiding and displaying themselves, and so they automatically moved out of his way, as, in a different manner, they also did for the waiters with their trays. Watching the process were the elder partners – the son, perhaps, had at last gone home. They watched with great earnestness, and when a woman in leopard skin came up to whisper something to the first partner, the other, increasing his concentration, could not resist stepping forward and standing like a mooring-post in the crowd – in case Sir Gerald should turn and need him.

Diana continued talking to the group around her, but was clearly conscious of Banks's tour of the walls. She contrived quick little glances behind her. Inside she must have been cursing Janos's behaviour of four years ago which still made it impossible for her (in her mind at least) to approach Sir Gerald directly.

The first partner, having satisfied the woman in leopard skin, turned and saw Janos standing beside me. His face was creased with smiles. Coming over he beckoned to Janos to bend his head down and listen.

'Four,' he said. 'Four large ones. We're very pleased. Would you like to come over and have a word with Sir Gerald Banks?'

'It is better he regards the canvases,' said Janos. And then added, 'We have known each other.'

The partner nodded his chin on his chest and, still smiling, sucked in his breath. "'Course, 'course. Just as you like, Mr. Lavin.'

He walked across into H—'s room to keep the irons hot there.

We both heard a woman's voice saying:

'I'm told he's Hungarian. And I must say I can feel a little of the same feeling as in Bartok, don't you?'

Janos was not a humorous man. He laughed, sometimes warmly, at other people's jokes; but he seldom made jokes of his own. His reaction to hearing this remark was one of the few occasions I can remember him being deliberately funny. All he did was to nudge me, and pull a face – a kind of idiot face with wide-open eyes and mouth, and imaginary straw hair nodding sideways in mock wisdom. Perhaps I found it funny because it was so unexpected, in a certain way so shocking, like seeing the first moment of an epileptic fit before one has realized what is happening. For ten seconds his face was quite inane. Then he stopped the imitation and lit a cigarette.

A man came up. Sir Gerald Banks passed, followed by third partner, into H—'s gallery. The man said:

'My name is Berkeley-Tyne. You're Janos Lavin, aren't you?' Janos nodded.

'You probably won't know my name, but I'm editing the new art monthly called Impact. I'd like to ask you a few questions about your work – which, incidentally, I like in part a good deal. Then we'll arrange to take some photographs.'

'Of me or the paintings?' asked Janos.

'The paintings.'

'Good. Who is backing this new magazine?'

'We're guaranteed by certain American museums. But naturally, in policy matters, we're quite independent.'

'I see.'

The man was young, large and going to fat a little. His manner was aggressive, but it was also direct. He obviously hated aesthetes. His hair was greased down and he wore dark, thick-rimmed glasses.

'You disapprove of all American museums?' he asked.

'No.'

'Let's start off from where we agree,' he said. 'You agree that in general today painting and sculpture are created and judged by standards that are basically nostalgic – outdated.' He spoke the last word with full managerial contempt.

180

'*I do not understand to where you are going,*' said Janos.

'*Take your own work. You're interested in the modern city. You're interested in the modern mass man. You're not very interested, I take it, in hand-made eccentricity. You like bikinis. You like scooters. You probably like jet aircraft and espresso bars. Good. But how many artists have this attitude, I ask you?*'

'*There are many modern things I do not like.*'

'*Such as?*'

'*Monopoly capitalism, flame-throwers. H-bombs, the yellow press.*'

'*Ah! But that is politics. And we're concerned with techniques.*' (He pronounced the word technics.) '*But to go back to your own work. You accept the realities of modern life. Implicitly you reject nostalgia. Or, rather, that is your intention. Actually – in my humble opinion – you make a dream of this modern reality and become nostalgic about the future!*'

'*Like the Jews in the Old Testament.*'

'*Exactly.*' The man took the remark entirely seriously. '*Your style proves this. It has nothing to do with modern technics.*'

'*No?*'

'*Have you ever used a commercial paint-gun?*'

'*No.*'

'*It suggests images of a totally new kind.*'

'*Yes?*'

'*Did you know that machine calculations can now give us answers to problems that no human mind can tackle?*'

'*No.*'

'*Furthermore we act on these answers. That is the token of the complexity of the mass civilization in which we live. The modern artist is going to face that complexity. And the only way he can do that is to share intuitively in every technic that makes up the fabric of his environment!*'

Mr Tyne did not allow himself gestures, but as he talked his round face became hotter and redder, and his words became increasingly clipped – as if being ejected like hot empty cartridge cases. Once or twice his hand came up to finger the slide-rule and pipe stuck in his breast pocket.

'*The truly modern artist has become an instrument. An instrument of measurement – though not in the Euclidian sense. His function is like the needle of a speedometer. He records the speed of the daily turnover of our mass-commodity-culture. But naturally there are no numerals on his meter. He invents his own signs to record the varying degrees of human stress, release, equilibrium. He represents the accidental factor, marking, say, the place where, under given circumstances, pleasure turns to pain, or, of course, vice versa.'*

A hand descended on Janos's shoulder and a thick voice chuckled: 'Janos, my old goat. Congratulations. Congratulations. Con – ' Harry had found him.

Janos turned round, looked amazed for a second, then recognized him and took his arm. As he did so, his expression was so confused that for a moment they both looked like drunks together standing there arm in arm.

Mr Tyne was in no way put out.

'We were discussing,' he said, 'how far the human factor expresses itself in the accidental.'

'Most unfortunately – nearly every bloody time – hence the birth-rate!' Harry ended this sentence on a high hiccoughing note that continued after the words were out, extended itself into a wheeze, and then, descending into his stomach, expanded into boiling laughter. Little tears came out of his eyes. His clothes shook. And his hands hung helpless at his side. Several people in the room turned round and looked at him with disturbed disapproval. The son of the third partner (who had evidently not gone home) hurried into H—'s gallery to find the senior partner who might act in this emergency. The laughter turned to coughing and Janos slapped Harry's back with one hand and supported him by the elbow with the other. Gradually the noise subsided. Harry's hands slipped down to his stomach as if to rearrange the weight there. Then, leaning towards Janos, he muttered:

'So sorry to leave. Back in the winking ... must piss.'

And walked, like a man blown by the wind, towards the stairs.

Mr Tyne still waited, managerial and persistent. Janos turned back to him, and was angry the only time that afternoon. One could see his bottom teeth, clenching, shove his whole head up with a jerk.

'In English, I believe you say – You know what you can do with your instruments.'

Mr Tyne smiled at the joke and waited. Only after Janos had turned his back did he realize the interview was over. Strolling across to the paintings, he examined them with ostentatious patience in order to prove, at least to me, that personal feelings count for little and that the editor of Impact *could always be counted upon to be objective. The galleries were now much emptier. The paintings were becoming visible again. The odd shock of seeing a life-size painted figure against a real one, was again possible. Even Diana had called it a day, and was now sitting in a chair in a corner talking to a woman friend, their hats occasionally touching as they nodded.*

Janos looked at his watch, waved at the Hancocks who were still too shy to come over to him, and indicated by mime that we should all go out and have a drink.

But at that moment both senior directors, one either side of Sir Gerald Banks, came back into the gallery. It was impossible to avoid the encounter, and it also immediately became plain that Sir Gerald had no wish to do so. He came straight towards Janos. Both partners left his side and formed a kind of V formation. The third partner, who was nearest to Diana, caught her eye and summoned her. Sir Gerald advanced. Janos straightened his back.

Banks was the heavier of the two, Lavin the wirier.

Banks held out his hand and said:

'*You never came to see my modern collection. But now you must — if only to see how your own paintings look in it.*'

He had gained, by surprise, a superb advantage.

'*What is the company?*' *Janos could do no more than parry.*

'*In general or in particular? I haven't decided which room to put your pictures in. But in general — the history-makers of this century and*' — *he smiled at Janos* — '*one or two eccentric favourites of my own.*' *He paused and looked round the gallery.* '*I would have bought that,*' *he pointed towards* The Waves, *his black stick and gloves carried in the same hand,* '*but I see the Holland Bequest have already got it.*'

'*Oh, but it isn't definite,*' *Diana said, half under her breath because she didn't want to say it, but audibly because the excitement of the day had finally made her reckless. Sir Gerald Banks looked at her disarmingly, guessing who she was. She was introduced and he said:*

'*I'm delighted to meet you, Mrs Lavin. I know the Bequest have only reserved that painting, but to tell you the truth I have another plan which I hope your husband will agree to.'*

Janos, only three feet away, stared in front of him. Sir Gerald continued to address Diana.

'The photograph of the painting called The Games *interests me very much. I have to go to Rome this week, but I wondered if, when I come back in a month's time, I could come and see it. Might I?' Suddenly turning his head, he addressed the direct question to Janos himself.*

'It is four metres by ten,' replied Janos.

'I know, I know. But did you see the old medieval hall when you came down? I'm having that done up now and turned into a room for little concerts and dances and so on. It could take some very large pictures.'

'Please make all arrangements you wish with my wife.'

Even Diana looked surprised at this complete abdication which appeared to be quite without sarcasm. I was more than surprised. Sir Gerald Banks, however, naturally took the remark at its face value.

'Thank you. I shall greatly look forward to coming.'

The two senior directors were looking as pleased as if they had also been invited to some exclusive ceremony. Reasonably so, for if Sir Gerald Banks bought The Games *they would collect their thirty-three per cent, and even if he did not, the fact that he had already bought two other paintings would favourably affect further sales. For example, when the director of the art organization, who introduced his daughter to me, came back and heard that Sir Gerald had bought two of Lavin's paintings, one of the crosses in his catalogue would quite likely be turned into a tick, or a tick would quite likely be underlined, and another painting would probably have been sold. I stared at them, one after the other. Both caught my eye and smiled back. I am sure they had quite forgotten my showing them a folio of Janos's work two years before. I am sure, because for them Janos had, as it were, changed his name since then. He had been, whatever his talent, A Painter-Among-A-Hundred-Thousand-Others. He was now, whatever his limitations, Janos Lavin.*

Banks was going. Pointedly he said au revoir *– and added his* *congratulations. He was a man of intelligence. He knew what could be bought and what could not.*

We were all very tired. The Hancocks stopped on their way out, excessively modest about taking up any of Janos's time. 'Just what you deserve,' Len kept saying, blinking behind his spectacles. As they left, Janos kissed Mrs Hancock's hand. The remnants of gestures were all that remained to him. He was exhausted.

H — strolled out of his room.

'Christ! Thank God that's over.'

He looked round the walls.

'My congratulations, Lavin. And the Holland Bequest. Where's it for?'

'Montreal, if they take it,' said Diana.

'Good. You've holed Montreal. I've got Melbourne and Chicago. Not so bad. Not so bad. Eh?'

He asked us all round to his club, but we made our excuses and went to a pub by ourselves. Just the four of us – the fourth being Max. After a few whiskies, we began to revive.

Indeed, Max and Diana became once more elated. They seemed to compete with one another in their enthusiasm about the day's success. Janos would have said that Max's enthusiasm was the result of his perverse pleasure in underlining in yet another way another of his own precious failures. This, I think, would only be half true. He was also straightforwardly delighted – as a man is delighted to see a large fire burning well, quite irrespective of whether it is his own or not. Max warmed and rubbed his hands at the afternoon's success and drank his whisky in the glow of it. Diana stared at the flames and screwed up her eyes, like an excited child at a night bonfire.

'Well,' said Max, 'you've made £2,000 in one day!'

Janos raised his glass in answering salutation. 'That is one way of putting it,' he said.

The street door of the bar banged open – so hard that we thought the glass had broken. We all turned round. Harry stood there. Leaning against the wall with his palms towards it, he edged his way in until the door swung back shut. He could clearly see nothing. Then, frowning with the effort, he focused his eyes and registered Janos. He tried to put out a hand to point at him, but as

soon as he let go of the wall he began to slide down it. So, instead,
he nodded at him.

'There, my friends' – his thick voice was just decipherable –
'you have the finest painter in Western Europe. Always said so.
Ever since I published his drawings. The finest artist of the – ' He
slumped to the floor and his head fell forward on to his chest. Janos
leapt forward as if the man had been shot. In fact, of course, Harry
was happy enough and unhurt. We took him back to the studio,
dumped him there on a bed, and went out and had supper.

OCTOBER II

My exhibition opened two days ago.

If we think of ourselves as special creators, we are wrong.
Everyone creates in the same way as we do. They invent,
imagine, hope, dream, frighten themselves, remember, observe –
and from all this they make for themselves certain ideas and
images, some expressible, some inexpressible. Where we're
different from most people is the way we try to destroy these
ideas and images. We hit at them, strike them, do our utmost to
kill them. We often succeed – the image falls away, lifeless, at
last recognizable as a lie or a cliché. Just occasionally there is one
that withstands our beating. It won't die. The more we beat it,
the stronger and harder it becomes. It becomes indestructible.
We have made a work of art – we, creators, whose job is to
destroy the tentative, the half-conscious, the merely evocative.
The strongest metal is tempered by successive heating and
cooling. All can heat – as a result of the great, marvellous
warmth of men. Our privilege, if that is what it can be called, is
that we can also cool – with the terrible coldness of our discipline.

This was the last dated entry in the sketch-book.

THE END

On October 16, a week after the opening of his exhibition, Janos disappeared. Diana came back to the studio in the afternoon and found only a note. It said he had to go away, and told her that if she needed money she was to take what the gallery owed him and, further, that she could sell any of his other paintings. The note added that she should get in touch with Max immediately. Diana thought this might mean that Max had some explanation. He had none.

Now, at the time of writing a year later, Diana and Max spend a lot of their time together and are clearly heading for an affair. My guess is that Janos foresaw this, that he realized that their unusual needs might well coincide (Max was a 'real refugee' and Diana could rescue him from his failure), and that he added his injunction in his note for this reason.

A fortnight after Janos's disappearance I received a letter from him:

Mon très cher ami,

I am happy to write you at last. Since I was leaving I have thought often about writing this note. I am no older. The old-looking hand is because I am in a train climbing eastwards. Outside it is dark and cold, but I begin to smell things that I never did smell in London. I wish I could send a packet of cigars.

I have not written before because I have not known what to tell. Until I reached Vienna I did not tell myself why I was here. Now, with the latest news in the journals, it is clear what I must do. So – I am in this train, looking with great suspicion at my fellow passengers. I have seen two other Hungarians. Both look as if they would take their mother's savings.

I will not be much use. I am old. And I chose my direction long past. Those who are not like I was will choose the same as I did. I go now to tell my mistake to those who are like I was.

Does this make sense to you? There was much we did not discuss together. But I will never forget your faith in my work. I had to voyage far to find that. Now that I travel in the opposite direction, do not think ingratitude. Simply the man in me reasserts himself. Opposite is a Viennese student – very pretty – round her neck she has tied a silly, gay piece of green chiffon – as she reads the chiffon bow tickles her chin – as I look at her she recrosses her legs. I have waited long enough, like a woman waiting to be courted.

Work well. We have little else. Trust your imagination a little more.

Please help Diana any you can about the paintings.

> *Courage, mon vieux,*
>> *toujours,*
>>> *ton*
>>>> *Janos*

Do you remember me telling you a story about being in a train and imagining the reflection of a police guard on the window? It has just happened again. He was, of course, a gentle ticket-collector!

What happened to him after this? We do not know. All our inquiries have proved negative. He may have been accidentally killed by a stray bullet. He may still be alive in prison. He may have changed his name, and so have become a man about whom we shall have news or shall read.

Even worse, we do not know what he did. Did he stand by and watch during those terrible days in Budapest? Did he join with the revisionists of the Petöfi circle? Did he fight side by side with those workers' councils who resisted the Red Army? Did he oppose this resistance and was he lynched by a mob as a Rákosi agent? Is he now a supporter of the Kadar government or does he bide his time? Each of these possibilities is reasonable. And the full tragedy of the Hungarian situation is revealed by the fact that we, who have the advantage of knowing some of this man's most intimate hopes, thoughts, confessions, cannot with any certainty declare which of these courses of action he was bound to follow.

We may use this confusion, this tangle of contradictions which strangled the life out of people, made simple men desperate and turned revolutionaries into counter-revolutionaries and vice-versa, we may use it if we wish to console ourselves. Diana is convinced that Janos was killed by Communists – by which she means the Hungarian Government. It is possible, but her choice helps her to forget that Janos may have voluntarily left her for good. The partners of the Malvern Gallery are convinced that, anyway, he is dead; he probably is, but, being dead, if a market is secured for his paintings, their prices will go up. George Trent is convinced that he was a Freedom Fighter; he may have been, but George is an independent young man fighting the Establishment who needs anarchic heroes. Max believes that he fled because he could not face the problem of what looked like the beginning of his success here. I rather doubt this, but even if there is an element of truth in it, it can only lead to further questions about the nature of that success. I myself would like to believe that Janos, if he is now alive, supports Kadar. Yet I can only see him outside the Malvern Gallery, standing in front of me and saying, 'Judge people as you have known them. Do not jump to conclusions.'

The only people who knew Janos well who are content to remain in doubt are the Hancocks. But then the Hancocks, like children, never speculate about anything that does not actually impinge upon their lives. They have accepted his departure as they would have accepted his being taken up to heaven in a chariot.

AFTERWORD
(1 9 8 8)

AFTERWORD (1988)

Paintings become more themselves with age. This is why the wish of certain restorers to clean a canvas until it is like what it was on the painter's easel the day he finished it is stupid, and dangerous for the painting in question. The transformation I'm talking about takes, on an average, about twenty years. I'm thinking of oil paintings – although I suspect an equivalent but less obvious process may effect watercolours, and even drawings. The change is a material one. The pigments settle into and onto the canvas. Their opacity or their transparency is modified. Their colours come together like parts of the same body. The painted image dries. Profoundly. The freshness and 'wetness' of each decision which once went into its making are replaced, for better or worse, by a sense of an inevitability beyond all decisions. If the painting is bad, it becomes so in an exemplary way; it becomes a warning. If it's good, it increases its authority.

Something a little resembling this process occurs even with clothes or shoes. Compare a new shirt in a shop window with the same shirt, newly ironed, in a wardrobe after it has been worn for a year. I'm not talking about any signs of wear and tear. I'm talking about it becoming a *fit*, about a subtle increase in its particularity and its *thereness*.

May the same thing be true of a book? If it is, the process is a more complicated one, for there is no simple material explanation.

I wrote this fiction over thirty years ago. If I open it and read a page today, it seems to me to be less questionable than when I wrote it. More certain of itself. Is this simply because my subsequent life has, as it were, grown over the wounds?

At that time I was thin, almost slight. My shoulders and chest hadn't yet broadened. I read Brecht and Camus. I went to visit Jack Yeats because I loved Ireland and the Irish. The wrongs done them will never be atoned for. I was at home with them. I rode motor-bikes. Everybody assumed I was a Communist Party member and I never denied it, for to deny it publicly would have been to play into the hands of the witch-hunters. I was mad about women and very shy. Probably few people saw my shyness, for I had a passionate dogmatic way of talking that covered up a multitude of hesitations. I lived near Monmouth and used to shoot rabbits. I had already been several times to East Germany and the Soviet Union. Nazim Hikmet was the poet I admired most – and perhaps the one I still do. I wasn't very convinced about my own talents as a writer but I was convinced that somewhere there was a demon or an angel looking after me.

A Painter of Our Time was not the first book I wrote – I had previously written a short monograph about the Italian painter Renato Guttuso, published in Dresden – but it was the first to appear in Britain. The publishers were Secker and Warburg.

Having delivered the manuscript, I anxiously awaited the editor's reactions. For years I'd been asking myself: Am I capable of writing a whole book or am I only a journalist, a writer of short pieces? I received a letter from Fred Warburg. He liked the book, he wanted to publish it.

The one favourable review the book received was by Peter Levi, S.J., in the Catholic weekly, *The Tablet*. The other reviews were catastrophic. Stephen Spender, in a prominent article in one of the Sunday papers, declared that such an evil book could only have been written by one other man apart from myself – namely, Goebbels when young.

Richard Wollheim in the magazine *Encounter* attacked me savagely for my alleged dishonesty and totalitarian sympathies. The critical reactions were so violent that Secker (who, at that time, were also publishing *Encounter*) decided to stop distributing the novel. After one month's life, my first book became a dead letter.

Perhaps today it is difficult to understand what prompted such violent reactions on the part of the establishment critics. On the last page of the book there is this supposedly tell-tale sentence. The narrator announces: "I myself would like to believe that Janos, if he is now alive, supports Kadar."

This one sentence was enough. The book came out in 1958. The Cold War was at its height, the CIA was in covert control of the magazine *Encounter*, McCarthyism was over but the fears it had manufactured were still around. Imre Nagy, the Hungarian prime minister of '56, had been executed in Budapest. The Geneva Accords were being sabotaged and the Diem regime set up as a separate state in South Vietnam. Conspiracies were being unmasked or hatched on every side. Each ruling clique or class was conspiratorially obsessed. And conspiracies, however devious their subterfuges or plans, invariably entail monstrous political and ideological simplifications. (This, incidently, is why secret services constitute a continual potential threat to democracy.) And here, in this paranoiac climate, was a narrator who admitted sympathy with the ENEMY!

I was fortunate. For that single sentence, if I'd lived in another country, I might have been sacked, or arrested for interrogation, or banished from the writers' union, or deprived of my passport. As it was I simply learnt early on in life a useful lesson. I learnt to acquire the pride that a modern writer needs to have here in face of the media – whether they lick or bite. Seven years later, after I'd written two more novels and when I knew that I could never stop writing, Penguin offered to bring out *A Painter of Our Time* as a paperback, and it was then that it became generally available to readers in Britain.

Early on, this first book of mine provoked another unexpected response, but this time an encouraging one. Through certain Hungarian friends a few copies of the original edition found their way to Budapest. One day I received a letter from Hungary, written by a woman who worked in the University. She said that although her subject was history she had a great love for painting, and so she was writing to me in London to ask where Janos's paintings might be found. I was amazed. The letter meant that the journal I had written for Janos was so convincing even to a Hungarian in Budapest (a city which, at that time, I had never visited), that she had taken it to be real.

This was another lesson. It confirmed to me that if you listened well enough, lent yourself enough to somebody else whose experience was totally different from your own, you could nevertheless speak for them and do so authentically. All storytellers knew this, of course, until the middle of our century. But then it began to be said – with increasing dogmatism – that nobody has the right to

197

write about anything they themselves have not lived. Fictional autobiography became the golden rule of the day. Thanks to an unknown woman in Budapest, I have never accepted this golden rule.

Twenty years later the novel was translated into Hungarian and published there. Now as I write, a television film of the book is in preparation as a Hungarian-British coproduction. Time passes...

About four years before I began working on the book (it took me three years to write it) I stopped being a painter. Somehow this book is a farewell to the art I had just abandoned. I gave up painting not because I thought I had no talent, but because painting pictures in the early '50s seemed a not direct enough way to try to stop the world's annihilation by nuclear war. The printed word was a little more effective. Today it is hard to make people realise how little time it seemed to us was left to prevent this ultimate disaster.

I started to earn my living by writing articles, including art criticism, for the press. Many of my friends and acquaintances remained painters, and my circle quickly widened as more and more artists responded to my writings about art. I spent a lot of my time in galleries and museums, but I spent even more visiting artists' lodgings and studios. Some of these artists were of my own age, but most were older, and a high proportion of them were foreigners – men and women who had come to Britain just before the war as political refugees from Fascism.

There was a prediliction on both sides, theirs and mine, a certain complicity. Based on what? Only in retrospect can I pinpoint it. It was based upon our experience of the English and the English refusal of pain. Pain is, by English definition, undignified. This is the starting point of all English philistinism. The European refugees and I (I in my relative naivety!) believed otherwise. Our complicity, our opposition, grew from the assumption that pain is at the source of human imagination. This didn't make us solemn – but it did make us embrace, make us put our arms around one another – to the embarrassment of any watching Englishman.

The life of these wandering years – wandering because I was continually visiting and because so many of my interlocutors were exiles – supplied me with the details of this novel. (When one *begins* to write fiction one clings to any given detail, like a ship-wrecked sailor to a spar on the open sea.) But it supplied me with far more than that. My exiled friends, often living in very poor circumstances, became my teachers about the world. (I never went to a university.) Above all they taught me about History and how one is obliged to live it. When I decided to write the book, I was entirely their pupil. But the voice for the book I had to find as my own, alone. So I was continually lying on my back on the floor of my room or somebody else's, shutting my eyes and waiting. At last a voice came – then voices.

Who was Janos Lavin? people ask me. The question supposes that the novel was a transcription from life, and perhaps this supposition is encouraged by the fact that the narrator was called John (like me) and was an art critic (like me). Yet no work of fiction is ever a transcription. Novels are never houses with portraits of real people in them.

It is to the theatre rather than painting that we should look for a clue about what happens when writing a novel parallel to a life. The novelist looks for actors to play the roles he is inventing. For example, in *A Painter of Our Time* I myself *play* an art critic who is not me. To play Janos Lavin I chose two actors, both close friends. The first was Peter Peri, a Hungarian sculptor of the same generation as Janos, and the second – for all the 'scenes' that involved painting – was Friso Ten Holt, a Dutch painter of my own generation.

I owe, as I imply at the beginning of the book, an enormous debt to both of them, for they played in my imagination with all their talents and principles, but they did not play themselves: they played a stranger called Janos Lavin who came to haunt me. Who he was I cannot tell you, any more than one can find a reason for love.

With the passing of thirty years, does anything particular or new about the book strike me today? Yes, rereading it now I suddenly realise that I have just finished writing the sequel to this book. It is a play, written in collaboration with Nella Bielski, and is entitled *Goya's Last Portrait*. Here too politics and art haunt each other. Another thing also strikes me about the novel today. I knew that it allowed the reader to enter into the preoccupations, solitude and dreams of a painter painting. The studio was filled with the life of an artist. What I didn't know was how politically mature the book is. Paradoxically it was exactly this which provoked such rage and jeopardised its first publication. There is nothing in it that I would want to change today. Time has confirmed its telling of a historical moment. What often dates the political content of a book is its opportunism. This book wasn't opportunist.

In saying that time has confirmed it, I do not necessarily want to suggest that it was prophetic. There are hopes for the future expressed in this book which may never materialise – as is the way with many hopes. Its maturity lies in its obstinate refusal to simplify the present, in its acceptance of the pain of heart-rending contradictions, and, despite all, in its quality of hope. It followed more faithfully than I realised the quotation from Gorky with which it began. And which, therefore, I repeat here.

Life will always be bad enough
for the desire for something better
not to be extinguished in men.

ABOUT THE AUTHOR

John Berger is one of Britain's – and our – most eminent art critics. He is also well known as a novelist, screenwriter, and documentary writer. His art books include *About Looking, Art and Revolution, A Sense of Sight, The Success and Failure of Picasso,* and *Ways of Seeing.* He now lives in a small French peasant community, where he is completing the third volume of his trilogy, *Into Their Labors* (which includes the already published *Pig Earth* and *Once in Europa*).